Table Of Contents

PREFACE xi

FOREWORD xiii

INTRODUCTION xv

CHAPTER 1
HISTORY OF HYPNOSIS 1
Magnetism 2
Early French Theorists:
    Somnambulism as Imagination 4
Early British Theorists:
    The Beginnings of Self Hypnosis 5
Animists vs Fluidists 6
The Abandonment of Hypnosis 7
Charcot: Hypnosis as Hysteria 8
Liébeault, Bernheim, and the Nancy School:
    Hypnosis as Suggestion 9
Return to Animal Magestism 11
Auto-suggestion and the Neo-Nancy School 11
Baudouin 12
Psychoanalysis and Hypnosis 14
Dissociation Theorists: Janet, Sidis, & James 15
Hypnosis as a Positive Mental Tool:
    Munro & Bramwell 18

Hypnoanalysis 19
Hypnosis Research:
    Modern Quests for Understandings 20
Indirect Hypnotherapy 26
Self Hypnosis Today 36

CHAPTER 2
SUGGESTION: DIRECT, INDIRECT, AND BEYOND 37
Spontaneous & Induced Suggestion 40
Suggestion as Focused Attention 42
Suggestion as Ideomotor Phenomena 44
Expectancy as a Factor in Suggestion 44
Suggestion in Context 45
Further Differentiation of Suggestion:
    Direct, Indirect, Efferent,
    Afferent, Immediate, & Mediate 46
Indirect Suggestion 48
Suggestibility & Hypnotic Susceptibility 53

CHAPTER 3
THE UNCONSCIOUS 57
Everyday, Out of Awareness Phenomena 58
Automatic Habits 59
The Unconscious as Set: Russian Set Theory 60
Associative Qualities of the Unconscious 63
Dreams: Free Flow of Images 65
Unconscious Expressed Through the Body 67
Unconscious as Intuition 67
The Necessity For Both Conscious
    & Unconscious 68
The Unconscious as Right Brain:
    An Oversimplification 69
Context, Environment,
    and Culture as Unconscious 73
Summary 76

CHAPTER 4
MIND & BODY 79
The Personal Equation 80

Principles of Self Hypnosis

Pathways to the Unconscious

Simpkins and Simpkins have prepared a book that takes a unique perspective on self-hypnosis. Their exercises are well designed to help readers communicate with their unconscious using both direct and indirect suggestion. Both professionals and laypeople will find *Principles of Self Hypnosis* an articulate, thoughtful, and imaginative approach to learning and creativity.

Stanley Krippner, Ph.D.
Saybrook Institute

FORTHCOMING 1991 FROM IRVINGTON PUBLISHERS
FRONTIERS OF CONSCIOUSNESS
A SERIES OF BOOKS, MANY ACCOMPANIED BY AUDIO AND/OR VIDEO CASSETTES
Series Editor: Stanley Krippner, PhD, Saybrook Institute

ON THE INSIDE OF ILLNESS
Suzanne R. Engelman
$29.95 Cloth

MIND BODY MEDICINE
Vol. I The Stages of Healing
Vol. II The Language of Healing
Lewis E. Mehl and Gayle H. Peterson
$19.95 each Cloth

SPIRITUAL DIMENSIONS OF HEALING
Native American Shamanism and Holistic Medicine
Stanley Krippner and Patrick Welch
$39.95 Cloth (includes audio cassette)

ALIVE & WELL
A Path for Living in a Time of HIV
Peter A. Hendrickson, Ph.D.
$12.95 Paper $24.95 Cloth
Audio cassettes also available:
Guided Imagery Exercises for Healing $11.00
Hatha Yoga for Health and Relaxation $14.00

SHAMANS OF THE 20TH CENTURY
Ruth-Inge Hienze, Ph.D.
$14.95 Paper $29.95 Cloth

The paper used in this publication meets the minimum requirements of American National Standard for Information Sciences—Permanence of Paper for Printed Library Materials, ANSI Z39.48-1984.

PRINCIPLES OF
Self Hypnosis
Pathways to the Unconscious

C. Alexander Simpkins PhD
Annellen M. Simpkins PhD

A volume in the Frontiers of Consciousness series
Series editor, Stanley Krippner

IRVINGTON PUBLISHERS, INC.
NEW YORK

Copyright ©1991 by Irvington Publishers, Inc.

All rights reserved. No part of this book may be reproduced in any manner whatever, including information storage, or retrieval, in whole or in part (except for brief quotations in critical articles or reviews), without written permission from the publisher.

For information write to: Irvington Publishers, Inc.,
Executive offices: 522 E. 82nd Street, Suite 1, New York, NY 10028
Customer service and warehouse: 195 McGregor St, Manchester, NH 03102

Library of Congress Cataloging-in-Publication Data

Simpkins, C. Alexander.
   Principles of self hypnosis : pathways to the unconscious / C. Alexander Simpkins, Annellen M. Simpkins.
      p.   cm.
   Bibliography: p.
   Includes index.
   ISBN 0-8290-2415-8
   ISBN 0-8290-2465-4 (Includes audio cassette)
   1. Autogenic training. 2. Subconsciousness. I. Simpkins, Annellen M. II. Title.
RC499.A8S58 1991
154.7—dc20   89-11190
                   CIP

First Printing 1991
1 3 5 7 9 10 8 6 4 2

Printed in the United States of America

We Dedicate This Book To:

Our parents, Carmen and Nat Simpkins for their faith and loving support, to our children, Alura and Alex, for their patience, forebearance, and willingness to experiment confidently with the techniques, and to our clients past, present and future, may they always continue to grow.

Acknowledgement

We thank our hypnosis teachers Milton H. Erickson, G. Wilson Shaffer, and Ernest Rossi for sharing their great wisdom and clinical acumen. We are grateful to Elizabeth Erickson for her corrections, advice, and support.

Expectancy and the Mind-Body Integration 81
Stress Theory 82
Gestalt Therapy: A Theory of Mind-Body Unity 85
Sensory Awareness 89
Body Therapies 90
Ideomotor Phenomena:
    Communication with your Unconscious Mind 91
Body Image 94

CHAPTER 5
STEPS TO SELF HYPNOSIS:
RAPPORT WITH THE UNCONSCIOUS MIND 97
Preliminary Exercises 98
The Trance: Self Hypnosis Series 103
Hand Levitation 108
Visual Imagery and Hallucination 110
Anaesthesia and Hyperaesthesia 112
Time Distortion 115
Summary 120

CHAPTER 6
THE UNLEARNING OF LEARNING,
AND THE LEARNING OF UNLEARNING 121
Learning Theories 121
The Conscious-Unconscious Balance 131

CHAPTER 7
CREATIVE LEARNING
AND PROBLEM SOLVING 137
Unconscious Resistance:
    Opening Your Mind to Change 138
Preventing Yourself from Change 140
The Positivity of Negativity 143
Bypassing Limits Through
    Creative Problem Solving 144
Creative Thinking 148
Judgment 149
Choosing a Hypnotist 150

CHAPTER 8
CHANGING PARADIGMS *153*
Sports: Achieving Your Personal Best 154
Weight Control, Impulse Control,
    and Regaining Positive Self Esteem 166
Pain Control: Expanding your Threshold
    for Discomfort..175
    a) Obstetrics & Surgery 181
    b) Headaches and Learning to Reduce Stress 183
Phobias, Fears, and Anxieties:
    Finding the Courage to Change 187
Smoking: An Example of Habit Change 193

CONCLUSION *198*

BIBLIOGRAPHY *199*

AUTHOR INDEX *211*

SUBJECT INDEX *213*

"Truth refines but does not obscure"
(Nathanial Stone Simpkins, 1836)

Preface

Self hypnosis is an art of inner communication which can be used for many purposes. This book is written for the professional who is interested in helping himself or his clients, using some hypnotic facilitation, and for the person who is interested in theory as well as developing skills in self hypnosis to bring about changes. We recognize that the professional is accustomed to a complex lexicon, but wherever possible, we have used simpler terminology so that the intelligent layman can understand. We hope that the professional will bear with some simplification of psychological theory and advice to laymen on seeking professional assistance. Although the exercises are directed to the person performing the exercise, the professional can use the exercises himself or adapt them for clients.

A vast encyclopedia of techniques and applications could be written, but such a ponderous tome would be overwhelming in a single volume. This book presents a particular approach to self hypnosis which emphasizes some aspects more than others. Creative generalization from one context to another is possible. Our intent is to set people on a path of self discovery to evolve their own resources, ideas, and inventive applications. We hope to continue with more volumes, to assist further in facilitating with hypnosis.

Meta-Instructions For Exercises

The book encourages the reader to experiment with exercises throughout the book. Many of the exercises have complex instructions which might seem difficult to remember. The greatest success will be achieved by reading the exercise through at least twice. Then set the book aside, find a comfortable and quiet place to sit or lie down, and try to do the exercise. Since these exercises are mostly directed toward the unconscious response, you do not need to remember every instruction. The unconscious tends to find its own way when given the opportunity. Repeat an exercise over a span of time for maximum results. The trance instructions in the earlier chapters should be practiced thoroughly to develop skills with self hypnosis before attempting the applications in Chapter VIII. These exercises are intended to have wider applications than the specifics. The reader is encouraged to be creative.

Although we have frequently used the masculine pronoun, we do so only by convention and intend to refer to men and women equally.

Foreword

by Ernest L. Rossi PhD

This book is organized around three well thought-out steps: theory is developed as the background throughout; exercises make the theory real; and finally, clear directions are given for specific clinical applications.

Not only do the authors give a complete and well developed history of hypnosis with an emphasis on self hypnosis, but they show how particular practices evolve out of different frames of reference.

Then, going on to my favorite area, the authors achieve a uniquely balanced integration in their presentation of direct and indirect suggestion. They do not make the mistake of thinking of indirect suggestion as a way of prevaricating in the therapeutic situation. Rather, indirect suggestions are used in the correct sense, the Ericksonian sense, of bypassing the ego's learned limitations and accessing inner resources. Even when these new resources are not fully available for the client, he can learn to access them himself. This becomes the core of what therapeutic trance is and remains faithful to the core creative essence of Erickson's thought. Instead of the classical misconception of mistaking suggestion for hypnosis, the therapeutic trance is a way of enhancing the client's sensitivity to the mind-body system. Once again, they are correcting another misconception following the Ericksonian idea of hypnosis as sensitivity to one's unconscious rather than simply suggestion.

Their work gains an extra dimension of reality through their use of exercises throughout the text. For every bit of theory they introduce an exercise to illustrate. For example, the different forms of suggestion are illustrated with exercises. Sensory awareness exercises follow theory of mind-body interactions. Hand levitation and warming or cooling are examples of kinaesthetic alterations. Exercises in inner imagery illustrate visual effects. Instruction in time distortion teaches other hallucinary experiences.

Finally, the authors present ways to apply the techniques developed in the book to common applications. They consistently use the therapeutic trance as the primary source for learning.

An unusually lucid presentation and integration!

Introduction

> It is that which we do know which is the great hindrance to our learning, not that which we do not know.
> (W.I.B. Beveridge)

There are many books written on hypnosis, but self hypnosis is unique, requiring special skills. The individual attempting it must be both the hypnotist and the subject simultaneously. Hypnosis involves giving up conscious limits in order to allow spontaneous unconscious responses to occur. Good rapport with the hypnotist allows for a comfortable permissive atmosphere in which this can take place. The dilemma for self hypnosis is how to voluntarily do the involuntary: to deliberately be spontaneous and have good rapport with your own inner self.

Most self hypnosis books deal with this problem by teaching the conscious mind to dominate the unconscious mind. In this book we will present conscious strategies as a means to learn how to experiment with your unconscious mind, unfettered by conscious restraints. You will learn to return to natural functioning with your unconscious and to co-operate with your inner needs in a healthy and positive way.

This approach to self hypnosis involves trance, using the unconscious functioning without intervention from the conscious mind at times, and deliberate conscious assistance at other times. Conscious, direct suggestion, unconscious, indirect suggestion, and free flow of associations without suggestions are incorporated as needed. (Chapter 2)

The unconscious mind is a reservoir of positive potentials with unexplored new materials as well as lost and forgotten abilities from earlier years. This method teaches recognition of unconscious response: to sense it and allow natural responses to occur. Receptivity to the unconscious requires a different kind of knowing from rational conscious knowing. This can be learned, just as one learns to differentiate feelings, meanings, colors or any other sense data. (Chapter 3)

The mind is in an integral relationship to the body. The unconscious is reflected in body gestures and facial expressions as well as inner experiences such as hunger, thirst, temperature, fatigue, pulse rate, etc. Thus, self hypnosis involves learning to work from different starting points. Beginning from body sensations can lead to relaxation and involuntary physical phenomena such as hand levitation, heaviness, and temperature changes. Corresponding images in the mind may occur spontaneously, leading to thoughts, ideas, and complex associated meanings. Mind to body approaches use the imagination and fixation of attention through vivid reliving of early memories, hallucinations, and free flow of associations. Body relaxation might be a by-product of a very enjoyable memory, for example. Chapter 4 develops the interactions.

Chapter 5 teaches the reader how to induce hypnosis in himself. Rapport with the unconscious mind in trance is developed to enhance sensitivities. There are numerous hypnotic phenomena which are possible. The reader is encouraged to experiment with many different hypnotic effects.

People often have difficulty transposing learnings they have in a hypnotic session into everyday life. They find the gap between thought and action difficult to bridge. Chapter 6 helps the reader to make the hypnotic learnings real, to put changes into action.

The mind often presents resistance to change. These resistances can be worked with and developed into strengths. Chapter 7 teaches the reader to bypass conscious limits through creative problem solving, while helping with defenses and resistances. All of the above considerations lead to techniques and their applications for specific purposes. Self hypnosis can be a practical tool both for target areas and to facilitate a more general constructive process within the individual. Chapter 8 gives step by step approaches to specific problems.

A Theoretical Paradigm

This approach to self hypnosis implies a theory of balance. Both the conscious and unconscious can be used for orienting, problem solving, and hypnotic work. The authors conducted a research project investigating whether therapy which attempts to make the unconscious become conscious is more effective than therapy which develops the unconscious and does not make this conscious. Generally, both methods tended to be equally effective. (Simpkins, 1983) leading to the inclusion of both conscious and unconscious work in self hypnosis. Individual differences can be taken into account as the reader learns about his or her own inner sensitivities, abilities, and needs. As abilities unfold, the reader can develop an openness to creative therapeutic process and thereby tap a positive reservoir of potential from within. By recognizing the possibility that abilities lie beyond what we know consciously, people can learn to cultivate creative moments (Rossi, 1979) leading to openness to new possibilities and new learnings. Better adaptations to problems and difficulties can then emerge.

People vary on how they respond to hypnosis, as our readers will discover. For some who are very suggestible, hypnosis will seem to affect them through the heightened suggestibility they discover. Hypnosis may be experienced as an ideomotor phenomenon; some will feel things develop in their bodies from merely an imagined thought. They may watch in amazement as their hand raises, seemingly all by itself. Others will feel as if they fall deeply asleep and remember nothing. Hypnosis occurs spontaneously and differently for each person, though there are many typical experiences.

Once you become familiar with your own personal response to hypnosis, you can broaden and evolve to learn other responses.

Self hypnosis facilitates constructive responses, self awareness, and better use of more potentials within each individual. Normally, people have routine patterns of thoughts, attitudes, concerns, and feelings. Like a television set receiving three channels, 8, 10, and 39, this becomes the limited spectrum of possibility for the television viewer. He will tune the television to these channels only, ignoring any other signals. Then, one day he becomes curious about new possibilities for input. He decides to put a large antenna on top of his house. Suddenly he receives many channels. What was previously experienced as static is now pictures, programs, and a number of new options if he chooses to tune them in. Similarly, the mind limits us to a certain range of experiences. Other mental events are either disregarded or experienced as meaningless static. Openness to the unconscious through hypnosis draws in more data and new perspectives. These new potentials may be integrated to expand the horizons of experience.

Rather than merely programming the mind like the traditional stereotype of hypnosis, one learns to sensitize, become aware, and fine tune the data received. Paradoxically, this can include an experience of desensitization or getting used to it, as will be shown later. Spontaneous response occurs rather than repetitive conditioning. Furthermore, self hypnosis invites the subject to interact with his own responses and to utilize them creatively.

In using this book, some readers may not want to start at the beginning with the theoretical section. Hypnosis is first and foremost an experience, and some might prefer to go directly to the exercises and learn about the theory of hypnosis later, matching individualized experience with the historical theories presented in Chapter 1. Others might find that experimenting with practical exercises from a firm theoretical orientation gives a helpful map.

The reader is encouraged to experiment with exercises throughout the book. Many people are independent individuals who want to work things out on their own. In the context of these experiments they can discover techniques and ways of helping themselves. However, some problems require the expertise of a professional, or some people do better with the guidance of a hypnotist or psychotherapist. Reactions to the exercises should be felt and thought about. It is the hope of the authors that many people will be able to find their own positive potential for growth and development through the use of this book.

Note: Be sure to read meta-instructions in the Preface before starting this book.

Chapter 1
History Of Hypnosis

Because the historical past, unlike the natural past, is a living past, kept alive by the act of historical thinking itself, the historical change from one way of thinking to another is not the death of the first, but its survival integrated in a new context involving the development and criticism of its own ideas.

(Collingwood, 1957)

Background for understanding self hypnosis arises out of the history of hypnosis itself. The idea of self hypnosis, though contemplated by some early theorists, was not actually put into practice until much later. The important historical theories of hypnosis which contributed to the understandings used today are reviewed with highlights of the discoveries about self hypnosis. The final sections of this chapter describe modern hypnosis and modern self hypnosis, showing how technique and applications evolve from theory. The reader is encouraged to look for the links and think about the consequences of each theory.

Phenomena resembling hypnosis have been known for centuries. An Egyptian papyrus dating about 3000BC described procedures identical to modern hypnosis. (Dorcus & Shaffer, 1945) These states were often surrounded with an aura of the mystical and supernatural. Hull, a famous behaviorist and researcher of hypnosis in the 1930's observed that hypnotism originated in magic much the same way that chemistry arose from alchemy and astronomy came from astrology.

Janet (1925), whose studies of *Psychological Healing* included a comprehensive review of hypnosis through the ages, traced the phenomena back many centuries. Even before hypnosis was isolated as a discipline of its own, Janet pointed out instances where the basic ideas of hypnosis were understood and described. He pointed to a quote from Malbranche which represents the beginnings of modern hypnotic theory.

Passionate persons arouse passions in us and make upon our imagination impressions resembling those with which these persons are affected...among these persons, an idea fills the mind so exclusively that they pay no attention to any other thing than that represented by these particular images.

(Janet, 1925:152)

Janet believed that the study of what would later be called suggestion was the foundation of experimental psychology.

Magnetism

Mesmer (1733-1815) was a medical doctor who is credited by some as being the major figure to popularize hypnosis. He was controversial and theatrical. His pamphlets portrayed him as being a dedicated man who arrived in Paris with a discovery that would put an end to human suffering. His downfall came in turning to the leading academic and scientific organizations of the country for support.

His medical dissertation (1766) was written on the influence of the planets upon bodies of men. He evolved the concept that the two halves of the human body act as poles of a kind of animal magnet. Disease results from an improper balance of magnetism. Animal magnetism was believed to be a gas or fluid which was under control of the human will. Mesmer believed that this fluid could be seen by the trained subject as it came streaming from the eyes and hands of the magnetizer.

Sickness, he maintained, resulted from an obstacle to the flow of the fluid through the body, which was analogous to a magnet. Individuals could control and reinforce the fluid's action by "mesmerizing" or massaging the body's "poles" and thereby overcoming the obstacle, inducing a "crisis" often in the form of convulsions, and restoring health or "harmony" of man with nature.

(Darnton, 1970: 4)

Because he was able to create such visible results, sending his patients into convulsion, many were convinced that he did indeed hold the key to a tremendous power. Mesmer and his followers emphasized the great influence the magnetizer had on the subject, lending a powerful and mysterious aura to the magnetizer.

One of Mesmer's disciples, Marquis de Puysegur, observed three central features of Mesmer's phenomenon: 1) the magnetized subject could only hear what the magnetizer said and was oblivious to all else. 2) The subject accepted suggestions without question. 3) He could recall nothing of trance when awake. This interpretation of Mesmer's theory implied that the patient was the passive recipient of the effects. Many of the modern conceptions about hypnosis derived from such views.

Mesmer was unsuccessful in gaining medical acceptance of hypnosis. The Royal Society of Medicine, the influential medical group of the period formed a commission to hear Mesmer's claims on hypnotism. They judged animal magnetism to be useless and dangerous. Darnton (1970), author of a study of Mesmerism as a phenomenon of pre-revolutionary France, claimed that Mesmer's system threatened the medical and academic establishment, and thus they rejected his ideas. Mesmer and his followers then appealed to the masses in pamphlets which alarmed the government by their claims that the privileged classes were trying to suppress Mesmerism's attempts to help the common man. Mesmer fled to Germany. The subsequent outbreak of the French Revolution stopped most investigations of Magnetism in France.

Early French Theorists: Somnambulism as Imagination

Despite Mesmer's failure to gain approval from the scientific community, interest in magnetism was not lost. In the early 1800's several Frenchmen were working with the phenomenon. These men quietly experimented in their own homes and offices as pioneers. Details of them as persons are lost in forgotten memories and the pages of rare books. Yet their theories have become the basis and background of modern hypnosis. These theorists considered it to be a form of sleep, and thus they called it "Somnambulism."

Bertrand (1820) believed that suggestion was the determiner of the state, not fluids or magnets. In his book, *Traite Du Somnambulism*, Bertrand described the movements, actions, and hallucinations which could be aroused in the mind of the somnambulist. Bertrand was one of the first to state that hypnosis, then called artificial somnambulism, was due solely to the workings of the imagination.

Delueze (1825) discussed anaesthesias, amnesias, and posthypnotic phenomena, some of the characteristic applications of hypnosis used today.

The Abbé Faria was one of the first to apply the idea of inducing somanmbulism by simply saying to patients, "I wish you to go to sleep." His work opened the possibility of instantaneous inductions, which is commonly used today. He worked with many people using somanambulism quite successfully.

Noizêt, a friend of Bertrand, wrote a book which makes the link between Bertrand and what was later to become the Nancy School. He stated:

> The fundamental psychological law which is at work is the law in accordance with which every idea tends to become an action; the suggested action is performed because the idea of the cation has made its way into the subject's consciousness.
> (Janet, 1925:157)

Artificial somnambulism was seen as a normal state working with the general laws of imagination, expectant attention, and desire. As the reader will see, self hypnosis can incorporate with benefit many of the concepts from this orientation to trance. Mesmer's mystical orientation was unnecessary for hypnosis. The door was opened for modern developments in the art and science of hypnosis and hypnotherapy.

Early British Theorists: The Beginnings of Self Hypnosis

Concomitantly to the French somanambulists, James Braid was working in Manchester, England with the same kind of phenomena which he named "Hypnotism" to differentiate it from Mesmerism. He was a conservative surgeon who carefully experimented and wrote, seeking always to give scientific meaning to his findings. This tended to narrow the gulf between himself and medicine while broadening the gap with Mesmerism.

Braid initially believed that sensory fixation of the eyelids was central to trance induction. The rolling of the eyes upwards causing a paralysis of the eye muscles brought on the phenomenon of hypnosis. Braid stated:

> It is this very principle, of over-exerting the attention by keeping it riveted to one subject or idea which is not of itself of an exciting nature, and overexercising one set of muscles, and the state of the strained eyes, with the suppressed respiration, and general repose, which attend such experiments, which excites in the brain and whole nervous system that peculiar state which I call hypnotism, or nervous sleep.
> (Braid, 1960: 30)

Braid produced trance in his family and friends by having the subject's eyeballs fixed in the same position and the mind riveted to the one idea of the object held above the eyes.

Eventually the eyes closed with a vibratory motion and the subject entered an altered state. At this point, the hypnotist could raise the subject's arms or legs and the subject would remain in this position. This is called catalepsy. Following this phase, Braid saw a deeply relaxed, refreshing sleep with no rigidity of the muscles. These observations proved to him that he had discovered a phenomenon different from Mesmerism.

Braid's earlier theory of hypnotism emphasized the importance of sensory fixation. "It is, however, but a step in thought from visual fixation to the fixation of attention." (Boring, 1950: 127) His later view was broader with a more psychological orientation. Braid was one of the first to consider the possibilities of self hypnotism. He cited experiments where patients hypnotize, manipulate, and rouse themselves. Braid simply asked them to rub their own eyes. They experienced the same results as those done by an operator. This proved, he believed, that hypnosis emanates from the mind and body of the individual and not from the power of the operator. This theory was quite contrary to the Mesmerists who saw the power as emanating from the operator. Mesmerists would wave a wand or gaze at the subject: the superstition of not looking into the eyes of the hypnotist for fear of being entranced derives from this.

Animists V. Fluidists

During these years (1840-1860) many people in both England and France worked with and theorized about hypnosis. A quarrel developed between two groups: The Fluidists and the Animists. The Fluidists believed changes in the subject are due to physical effects of fluids emanating from the magnetizers, whereas the animists said everything depended on the changes induced in the subject's mental states. To the Animists, physiological changes were obtained through mental action.

Abandonment of Hypnosis

James Esdaile, an Englishman in India, performed thousands of minor operations and 300 major surgical procedures using hypnosis as the only anaesthesia. The British government proved to be more open-minded than the medical profession.

> A letter to the Medical board describing his work remained unanswered, but a later report to the government, after he had more than 100 cases to describe, led to the appointment of a committee of investigation. The report of the committee was cautious but favorable to further research, and the government accordingly in 1946 established a small Mesmeric hospital in Calcutta where Esdaile might continue his work.
> (Boring, 1950: 123)

Although the funding from the Indian government did not last long, official visitors to the hopital were convinced that Mesmerism was effective as an anaesthetic and partially effective in reducing operative shock. Esdaile eventually left India because of the climate but continued his active interest in Mesmerism.

With the discovery of ether in 1846 and chloroform in 1847, the use of hypnosis for anaesthesia was abandoned. For 20 years hypnosis was mainly conducted by charlatans or else performed secretly. Reputable scientists no longer dared openly study hypnosis since the phenomenon was considered fraudulent.

Ironically, people were slow to accept the usefulness of ether and chloroform. In fact, P.T. Barnum and others exploited nitrous oxide for theatrical show. Erickson (1961) pointed out the paradox that during the period when hypnosis was popular, exploiters were pushing anaesthesia. Over the more recent decades the reverse has been true, where anaesthesia is the accepted mode in medical use and hypnosis is often exploited by charlatans.

Charcot: Hypnosis as Hysteria

Charcot, founder of the Salpêtrière (1825-1883) school was a physician who treated nervous disorders. He attempted to research hypnosis strictly scientifically, as he had done throughout his medical career. His work narrowed the study of the phenomenon to observable physiological manifestations, the movements and reflexes of the subjects. He considered the psychological dimension dangerous and unscientific, calling this "Minor Hypnosis". His view is reminiscent of the early behaviorist stand toward psychotherapy where only observable behaviors were considered scientific material. Mental experiences were unscientific and therefore inadmissible.

The province which Charcot observed and classified was called "Major Hypnosis." He developed exact classifications of phenomena according to the following reactions:

1. Lethargy—eyes closed, profound slumber, unresponsiveness
2. Catalepsy—eyes suddenly open, limbs retain any position imposed by experimenter
3. Somnambulism—subject can hear, speak, and manifests readiness to accept suggestions.

Charcot's research was based upon work with his patients. The best subjects proved to be female hysterics. This led him to believe that hypnosis was a pathological state. Despite or perhaps because of this cautious conception of hypnosis, Charcot was able to gain acceptance for his hypnotic research in 1881 from the same academy who had rejected Mesmer years before. This decision broke down the condemnation of hypnosis and allowed practitioners to come out of hiding.

Liébeault, Bernheim, and the Nancy School: Hypnosis as Suggestion

Liébeault was a humanitarian, providing free medical hypnosis to thousands of patients suffering from many physical symptoms. He is considered by some to be the real father of modern hypnosis. He believed that hypnosis could favorably influence both functional and organic disease. He claimed cures for numerous physical disorders. Bernheim, a professor at the Nancy School, heard of Liébeault's claims and was so incensed that he went to his clinic to expose him as a quack. Instead, he was amazed by Liébeault's work and undertook a study of hypnosis which became a major dedication for his life. His books which followed from his studies with Liébeault and his own research became the foundation of a major movement in hypnosis, the Nancy School.

Bernheim believed that the whole explanation of hypnotic phenomena lies in suggestion. He defined suggestion as the influence exerted by an idea which has been suggested and received by the mind. The phenomenon occurs automatically, without thinking about it. Everyone experiences this daily: when someone mentions a tart lemon we automatically salivate. Bernheim called these phenomena instinctual acts. "It is impossible to be seized by a vivid idea without the whole body being placed in harmony with this idea." (Bernheim, 1973:129) People experience this continually, with characteristic facial expressions and body gestures which automatically accompany emotions. An idea which initiates in the mind automatically gives rise to a corresponding sensation in the body. This central concept in Bernheim's thought marks the origination of the Ideomotor Theory, central to hypnosis and self hypnosis today.

Bernheim believed that during the hypnotic state the mind is dulled, attention is distracted and automatic responses occur involuntarily. In trance, the subject's transformation of thought into action, sensation, movement, or vision is so quickly and actively accomplished that rational or intellectual inhibition has no time to act. Unlike some hypnotists who thought that conscious activity is completely paralyzed, Bernheim saw the ego involved as an observer. For example, a patient in hypnosis could not open his eyes. Upon awakening he said he heard everything but could not prevent his hands from raising and his eyes from closing. Bernheim strongly held that weakening of the will is not the central force in hypnosis: rather, the mechanism of suggestion is the determiner.

> There is an increase of this reflex ideomotor, ideosensitive, and ideosensorial excitability. With hypnotism the ideo-reflex excitability is increased in the brain so that any idea received is immediately transformed into an act, without the controlling portion of the brain, the higher centers, being able to prevent the transformation.
> (Bernheim, 1973: 138)

Bernheim compared hypnosis to sleep in that sleep favors the production of suggestions by suppressing or weakening the moderating influence. He theorized that sleep, whether artificial (hypnosis) or spontaneous, is a cerebral condition in which the reasoning faculties can be focused upon a class of ideas. What dominates is this fixation of the nervous system upon an image or idea suggested.

Bernheim had a theory of posthypnotic suggestion as well. Posthypnotic suggestion involves the carrying out of suggestion given during trance when the subject wakes up. He believed that the hypnotic subject is conscious of what he was doing while asleep. However, once awake these thoughts are effaced. They remain latent and recallable when back in the somnambulistic state. Posthypnotic suggestion is experienced as a new idea when executed. Actually, the subject has lost the memory of the idea he had in trance. The suggestion is stored in the mind during sleep and remains as a latent memory upon awakening, susceptible to being conscious again spontaneously.

Bernheim worked with hundreds of hypnotic patients. The Nancy School inspired many others to work in hypnosis and firmly established it as a therapeutic method.

Return to Animal Magnetism

Animal magnetism reappeared with Alfred Binet (also author of the intelligence tests): and Charles Feré's book, *Animal Magnetism*. They performed careful research projects empirically testing the effects of magnets on hypnotic subjects. They magnetized patients with a hidden magnet and trance occurred. They used wooden magnets and nothing happened. They believed that the element of suggestion and expectant attention had been removed by their experiments. These and many other empirical tests convinced them that suggestion had nothing to do with hypnotic effects.

Modern research in expectancy has shown that experimenter bias can alter results even if the experimenter tries to appear neutral. This may have had an influence on their findings. However, in a recent study, the experimenter used the passing of hands method of magnetism and found that deeper trances occurred with this method than when traditional hypnotic techniques were employed. (Pulos, 1980) This raises questions for further research.

Auto-Suggestion and the Neo-Nancy School

Thus far, self hypnosis had not been explored, with the exception of Braid's work in the early 1800's. Braid viewed hypnotic phenomena as occurring in the mind of the subject, not as coming from the operator. These ideas, though not inconsistent with Bernheim's theory were not developed or used in the Nancy School.

Emil Coué was influenced by Liébeault and in 1923 founded the "Neo-Nancy School." As a druggist, he spent many years giving suggestions to accompany his customers' drug orders. He spent 25 years observing and thinking about the positive results he observed from his suggestions. Finally, at age 55 he came out with an approach which abandoned trance entirely and worked with waking auto-suggestion. His method was based on consciously harnessing the effects of the imagination. He distinguished between will power and imagination. He taught patients to vividly imagine each morning, "Day by day, in every way I am getting better and better." He encouraged people to imagine the positive results they wanted to achieve and stop trying to will themselves to accomplish it. (See Chapter 2 for more detail.)

Coué believed that we have two selves: the conscious and the unconscious. The conscious possesses an unreliable memory while the unconscious self recalls perfectly, in minute detail. The unconscious regulates the functioning of all our organs and acts as mediator of all our functions whatever they are. This is synonymous with imagination, which always makes us act.

The key to directing the unconscious mind oneself is through the use of auto-suggestion. Suggestion is defined as the act of imposing an idea on the brain of another. But Coué believed that suggestions are only effective if the subject transforms it into an auto-suggestion. Many modern self hypnosis practitioners apply these same principles today.

Baudouin

Charles Baudouin developed a theory of auto-suggestion and self hypnosis drawn from Coué's theory of auto-suggestion but including trance. His book, *Suggestion and Auto-Suggestion* is one of the few which develops an indepth theory of self suggestion.

He defined the suggestion as the subconscious realization of an idea. This takes place in three phases:

1. The idea of a modification
2. The work of realization which occurs unconsciously
3. The appearance of the modification that has been thought.

People give themselves auto-suggestions constantly throughout their day without realizing it. These auto-suggestions act to influence what a person can or cannot accomplish. This influence works according to three laws. First, the "Law of Concentrated Attention" states that if spontaneous attention is concentrated on an idea, it tends to realize itself. Spontaneous attention is like that of a child, or when a bright color catches the eye. This is distinguished from voluntary and reflective attention where one is focused on something by choice.

The second law, the "Law of Auxiliary Emotion" holds that when an idea is enveloped in a powerful emotion, there is more likelihood that this idea will be suggestively realized. This occurs because spontaneous attention is closely associated with and dwells upon anything which is emotionally drawing or compelling.

The third law, the "Law of Reversed Effort" was one of Coué's most important contributions according to Baudouin.

> When an idea imposes itself on the mind to such an extent as to give rise to a suggestion, all the conscious efforts which the subject makes in order to counteract this suggestion are not merely without the desired effect, but they actually run counter to the subject's conscious wishes and tend to intensify the suggestion.
> (Baudouin, 1921: 137)

Because of the "Law of Reversed Effort," it is impossible to give an auto-suggestion without creating a negative counter-suggestion. Baudouin stated:

> Whenever we concentrate voluntary attention on an idea, which implies making an effort, I am simultaneously conscious of an action toward this idea, and of a resistance in consequence of which the idea continually escapes me...Thus when we concentrate on an idea, we do not think a single idea but two conflicting ideas which result in two conflicting suggestions which neutralize each other.
> (Baudouin, 1921: 146)

The problem becomes, how can a person make a voluntary effort to change? Baudouin found the solution in self hypnosis. During hypnosis one is relaxed and yet focused. Under these circumstances which he calls "contention" one can make suggestions which will be accepted without the reverse occurring to counteract it. Baudouin gave detailed instructions on going into an auto hypnotic state followed by self administration of auto-suggestions. His approach assumes that trance is fixation of attention. Once the consciousness is riveted on a single idea as in trance, the reverse suggestion cannot take hold.

Psychoanalysis and hypnosis

Breuer introduced the psychoanalytic applications of hypnotic therapy. He felt that the emphasis of hypnosis had been direct symptom removal. With his patient, Anna O., Breuer discovered that the original trauma relating to her hysterical symptoms could be brought out in hypnosis, resulting in cure. Janet simultaneously arrived at the technique of liberating repressed emotions associated with traumatic memories, although Breuer is given credit for the discovery.

Freud studied and used hypnosis extensively with patients. He published a book with Breuer, entitled *Studien Uber Hysterie*, in 1895. They stated:

> The individual hysterical symptoms immediately disappeared without returning if we succeed in thoroughly awakening the memories of the causal process with its accompanying affects, and if the patient circumstantially discussed the process in the most detailed manner and gave verbal expression to the affect.
>
> (Wolberg, 1948: 11)

They concluded that hysterical symptoms developed as a result of experiences so damaging to the individual that they were repressed. Hypnosis was helpful in bringing the repressed material into the open and thereby curing hysterical symptoms. Freud studied with Charcot and was so excited by the phenomena that he translated Bernheim's book.

Over the years Freud abandoned his earlier views, conceiving of the symptoms as not only manifestations of repressed instinctive strivings, but also representing defenses against these strivings. This led him to an emphasis on the irrationality of the use of hypnosis for removal of symptoms. His negative stand on hypnosis from the psychoanalytic orientation put a severe damper on interest in hypnosis. Kline points out that Freud's rejection of hypnosis had little to do with a questioning of the potency or validity of hypnosis as a psychological tool, but rather was a recognition of the difficulty in incorporating it into the therapeutic process. Freud's rejection was based upon:

> His difficulty inducing the hypnotic state in a high percentage of patients, inability to produce and maintain posthypnotic reactions of a therapeutic nature, and the intensification of both transference and countertransference reactions elicited through the hypnotic relationship.
> (Kline, 1958: viii)

> Very few people stayed with hypnosis, most notably Janet in France, Bramwell in Great Britain, and Prince and Sidis of the United States. Generally, hypnosis and self hypnosis took on a minor importance.
> (Wolberg, 1948)

Dissociation Theorists: Janet, Sidis, & James

Janet believed that the abandonment of hypnosis arose out of the controversy between the Salpêtrière School and the Nancy School. Charcot had given hypnosis medical acceptance by delimiting it to a physiological affect, thus placing it within the province of the medical profession. Bernheim's school saw it as a mental phenomenon which meant it fell under the psychological realm. Although the Nancy school was victorious, the win was at great cost to hypnosis. Psychology had no credibility to the medical field and thus hypnosis could not be worthy of study by practitioners. Research and practice of hypnosis declined for many years. Those who did work with hypnosis concerned much of their theorizing with attempts to reconcile the dispute between the Salpêtrierè and Nancy Schools.

Nonetheless, Janet continued to uphold hypnosis as an effective mode of treatment for neurosis. He stated,

> If my work is not accepted today, it will be tomorrow, when there will be a new turn to fashion's wheel, which is going to bring back hypnotism as surely as our grandmother's styles.
> (Janet, 1925: 151)

Janet was a central figure in the history of hypnosis, influencing many with his books. He theorized that complexes of ideas exist split off or "dissociated" from the personality. Through hypnosis these dissociated thoughts and experiences could become part of the consciousness once again.

Janet believed that hypnosis was not a state of sleep, nor should it be characterized as suggestibility. Hypnosis belonged to the group of somnambulisms, that is, modification of the mental state in an unbalanced individual. The modification was considered a temporary state in which the individual's personal memory is dissociated. Hypnosis not only arrests the normal personality, but also develops other tendencies which vary from person to person. (Janet, 1924)

He believed that one way we can discern the difference between a state of hypnosis and a normal state is that hypnosis involves a modification of personal memory whereas in everyday life personal memory is continuous. He cites an example: though he might be tired and depressed, he still remembers how he felt earlier when he was not feeling tired and depressed. But in trance these conscious balances and tendencies are replaced by repressed tendencies. These can be another life, another character, another memory that is evoked in place of the usual conduct. This can be useful in working with neurosis since it gives the patient an opportunity to experience something apart from his everyday tensions and problems. Secondly, hypnosis can activate dissociated parts of the personality which Janet called "tendencies".

Ordinarily, unused tendencies atrophy. During trance these tendencies can be reintegrated into the waking personality. (Janet, 1924: 147)

Sidis (1899) attempted to unify the views from the Salpêtrière and Nancy Schools:

> With the Nancy School, we agree that suggestion is all-powerful in hypnotic trance; the hypnotic trance is in fact, a state of heightened suggestibility, or, rather of pure reflex consciousness; but with the Paris School, we agree, that a changed physiological state is a prerequisite to hypnosis, and this modification consists in the disaggregation of the superior from the inferior centres, in the segregation of the controlling consciousness from the reflex consciousness.
> (Sidis, 1899: 70)

Sidis carried on Janet's perspective on hypnosis as dissociation. The higher conscious levels of controls were dissociated from the reflexes and automatic lower levels. During hypnosis the normal course of an idea is inhibited; a suggested movement or idea is carried through without interruption from the conscious mind.

William James was also influenced by Janet's hypnotic theory. In the normal waking state people have their consciousness and their subliminal consciousness. "In hypnosis, waking consciousness is split off from the rest of the nervous system while subliminal consciousness is laid bare and comes into direct contact with the external world." (James, in Taylor, 1982: 24) This secondary consciousness is intelligent as well, attending to its own concerns without interfering with active consciousness. Everyday awareness could be but an extract of a vast and greater reality which is "beyond the margin." (Taylor, 1982: 42)

Unlike Janet, James believed that suggestibility was the main "symptom" of hypnosis. In trance the subject develops motor efficacy. This means an idea can be translated with ease to muscular activity as ideomotor and ideosensorial excitability. Suggestibility causes a narrowing of the field of consciousness by introducing an idea which produces an intense emotional response. All other ideas are banished, creating a state of focused concentration.

James's hypnotic theory anticipated many of the ideas in modern hypnosis when he stated that the unconscious mind is a reservoir of untapped potential beyond the limits of conscious awareness.

Hypnosis as a Positive Mental Tool: Munro & Bramwell

The early 1900's marked a period when the medical model predominated and psychotherapy was struggling to become accepted as a viable mode of treatment. Some doctors saw the importance of the mind and attempted to persuade the medical profession to include the mental processes in their work. Munro was a medical doctor who lectured to other doctors around the country about the value of what he termed "Suggestive Therapeutics." He tried to show that psychotherapy could be an important adjunct to clinical work which doctors should recognize and use to improve their effectiveness.

For Munro, psychotherapy was synonymous with hypnosis and suggestion, occurring through three basic methods: 1) Hypnotic suggestion 2) Suggestion in the waking state, and 3) Persuasion, reasoning, or re-education. He stressed that it is of vital importance for all good physiological treatment to be accompanied by teaching patients healthy habits which unify mind and body. He was a forerunner of the concept of Preventive Medicine. Throughout all his work he emphasized the value of being an ethical physician committed to the welfare of his patients.

Suggestion was central to Munro's view. In order for a suggestion to be assimilated as a self-suggestion, one needs a mental attitude of conviction.

> This mental attitude evokes or calls forth latent powers or inherent psychic activities, and renders the reserve energy available or useless as he has confidence or lack of confidence.
>
> (Munro, 1911: 145)

Energy reserves could influence physiological processes and help in healing the body. Suggestion along with a positive mental attitude could promote healing and health, similar to positive thinking approaches popular today. Herbert Benson is a modern theorist who has championed and researched these issues in depth. (Benson, 1975, 1979)

Bramwell helped revive the concept of self hypnosis. He pointed out that "The essential characteristic of the hypnotic state is the subject's far-reaching power over his own organism. (Bramwell, 1903: 437) He revived applications to medicine and described various theories, sympathizing with Braid. In his final assessment he notes that hypnotic phenomena leave many unanswered questions, but he was hopeful that hypnosis could help in curing and preventing disease, alleviating pain, giving sleep, and improving moral states. (Bramwell, 1903: 439)

Despite the efforts of Munro and others, most physicians of the day considered hypnosis to be as primitive and unscientific as blood-letting and leeching. Once again, hypnosis was disregarded as beneficial. Not until World War I, when many soldiers suffered from the trauma of war, was hypnotherapy revived to perform brief therapy. Many excellent accounts of successful treatment were given during this period which led to a renewed interest in hypnosis.

Hypnoanalysis

Controversy continued as to the real value of hypnotherapy. Some began to use it for what Hadfield coined, "Hypnoanalysis." Patients were put into trance and regressed to a time period when a damaging experience occurred. They were encouraged to relive the event and to liberate the associated emotions.

One of the most famous accounts of hypnoanalysis was made by Lindner who hypnoanalyzed a criminal psychopath. He tape recorded all the sessions and carefully recounted the treatment process. The patient relived traumas which he endured as an infant. Lindner described the process as:

> Equivalent to a surgical removal of barriers and hazards, that it pierces the psychic substrata and raises the repressed to the level of awareness.
>
> (Wolberg, 1948: 16)

Wolberg wrote several comprehensive volumes on hypnoanalysis and medical hypnosis. He divides hypnotic phenomena into induction phase, trance phase, and post hypnotic period. His knowledge of the many historical theories and research on hypnosis is comprehensive. Thus, his own view takes into account the great complexity of the subject. He believes that trance cannot be explained by exclusively psychological or physiological theory alone. Rather, he sees it as a complex psychosomatic reaction which includes both the psychological and physiological. The physiological aspect involves critical inhibition (see Pavlov's theory to follow), that is, suspension of activity of the higher brain functions and a linking of the ego to subcortical systems. The hypnotic subject can actually control various organs and somatic functions more directly than in the waking state, which explains some of the phenomena which occur in hypnosis.

Wolberg emphasizes hypnosis as an analytical process whereby the patient is led on a journey of self discovery. Through regression, revivication, and the ability in trance to explore unconscious experiences, the patient can bring up difficulties and work them through for a healthier level of functioning.

Hypnosis Research: Modern Quests for Understanding

Hull

Hull (1933) attempted to give a scientific account of hypnosis through the modern experimental method. He felt that the lack of clinical attention to hypnosis in the 1900's had been an advantage, since clinical work was impossible to quantify and measure. He believed that careful research could give hypnosis acceptance from the scientific community as well as answering some of the many unanswered questions about the nature of hypnosis.

Hull tested many aspects of hypnosis. He set up a laboratory at Yale University. There he performed hundreds of experiments on suggestion and waking suggestion. He tested some of the conflicting theories: hypnosis as dissociation, hypnosis as sleep, and hypnosis as habit.

Hull's work led him to draw certain conclusions about hypnosis. He found rapport to be an inherent and essential characteristic of hypnosis. He also found that hypersuggestibility characterized hypnosis. He believed that the change in suggestibility was a measurable verification of hypnosis. He thought that he disproved several beliefs held from the past by finding that hypnosis was not a form of sleep, nor was it a pathological condition related to hysteria, nor was it a state of dissociation.

Pavlov

Pavlov, the Russian researcher who was famous for his formulations of stimulus-response conditioning also did extensive studies of hypnosis. He formulated a physiological theory. Pavlov found that the cerebral cortex influences the entire organism in a complex manner he called the primary signaling system. All animals have this signaling system which maintains the balance between the organism and its environment. Man distinguishes himself from animals through what Pavlov called the secondary signaling system of higher thinking and speech. The "Word" is an actual conditioned stimulus which affects the processes of man's higher nervous activity. One man's words can powerfully affect another:

> A word is as real a conditioned stimulus for man as all the other stimuli in common with animals, but at the same time more all-inclusive than any other stimuli.
> (Platonov, 1959: p.15)

This influence of a person's words over another can only take place after there has been a conditioned stimulus. For example, the word "hurt" acquires definite meaning for a child only when it is combined with real pain at least once. The verbal stimulus of the word can actually replace the action of the pain whereby the mere mention of it brings on a pain response.

Pavlov defined hypnosis as a form of sleep. Based upon numerous experiments with animals Pavlov concluded that sleep is brought on by the higher division of the central nervous system. When there is exhaustion of the cortex during the waking state, a condition of inhibition replaces the excitation giving the cells a chance to be restored. Natural sleep, like hypnosis, is the process of such internal inhibition spread over the entire cerebral cortex. Partial sleep occurs when the individual parts of the cerebral cortex undergo inhibitory response while others do not. Broken up or scattered sleep takes place in an even more isolated manner. Pavlov thought this accounts for the different levels of hypnosis which occur.

Suggestion and auto-suggestion are based upon the transition of cortical cells to an inhibitory state. A suggestion or auto-suggestion actually stimulates a reaction in the brain which brings about an hypnotic sleep reaction whether the subject knows it or not.

Due to limitations of space and time we must simplify much of Pavlov's complex theory. Recent physiological research indicates other approaches may be more fruitful.

Hilgard

Hilgard has been involved in hypnotic research since 1957 and has written and researched prolifically in the field of psychology for decades. He states that his interest in hypnosis was:

> To see hypnosis "domesticated" as a part of normal psychology, on the assumption that understanding of the normal human mind and behavior will be en-

hanced if hypnosis is taken seriously along with perception, learning, motivation, and the other accepted topics of general psychology.

(Hilgard, 1977)

His research has integrated hypnotic understandings in with motivation, learning, memory, and perception. He is well known for development of the Stanford Hypnotic Susceptibility Scales. The relative hypnotizability of an individual can be determined based upon their scores on this series of suggestibility tests. Hilgard found in his research that a certain percentage of people have genetic talents with hypnosis, similarly to how some people are athletically, musically, or artistically gifted. This view differs from Erickson who believed that all people can be trained to be hypnotized despite different hypnotizability ratings.

Hilgard explored Janet's ideas on dissociation and developed a neodissociation theory. He differed from Janet by removing the neurotic hysterical component. Hilgard found that all people, healthy and neurotic alike, always experience more than one thing at a time. In hypnosis this is exaggerated and can thereby serve as an arena for deepening our understanding of the workings of attention, memory, perception, creativity, imagination, etc. Hilgard hypothesized that people have what he called a "hidden observer." Even though a person thinks he does not recall anything about an experience in trance, there is a part, a hidden observer, which does indeed recall everything. Dissociation is also central in pain control, for which he carefully researched and developed applications.

Hilgard believed that hypnosis is a state in and of itself. His many research subjects were able to differentiate a distinct experience of trance which convinced him that trance is more than suggestibility, though heightened suggestibility is part of it. Through his many years of careful research Hilgard has influenced the course of hypnosis. He has led it away from the weird, the mystical, and the neurotic into the realm of the psychological.

Orne

Orne, another important researcher of hypnosis theorized that hypnosis is a state. He attempted to demonstrate this empirically in a series of experiments. His research showed that "reals" demonstrated higher tolerance to pain, performed posthypnotic acts more readily, and were dehypnotized more slowly. He differentiated the genuinely hypnotized subject from the hypnotic simulator by what he called "Trance logic." Erickson also found the logic of the hypnotized person to be different from that of the waking person. Orne theorized that hypnotic subjects are influenced by environmental expectations which he called the "demand characteristics" of the situation. His work indicated both a psychological and sociological basis for hypnosis. The Hopkins research experiments on psychotherapy utilized this as one of the bases for understanding similar effectiveness ratings among apparently widely differing approaches to psychotherapy. (Frank, Hoehn-Saric, Imber, Liberman, Stone, 1978)

Sarbin & Coe

Several researchers (Sarbin, Coe, and others) have offered a different perspective on hypnosis as one form of role-taking. Sarbin believed that a theory of hypnosis must account for four major phenomena: dissociation of behavior, automatic response, how such a magnitude of response can follow from mere spoken instructions, and individual differences in response to hypnosis. The role-taking theory when enacted at a very high level of organismic involvement explains these hypnotic phenomena. Successful role-taking depends upon favorable motivation, role perception, and role-taking aptitude. Similarly, a successful hypnotic subject is highly motivated, has a clear perception of how he should act as a hypnotic subject, and wants to be involved in this role. He states that this view of hypnosis removes the "magical" element and makes it explainable, measurable, and understandable.

Barber

Barber, another contemporary theorist and researcher contends that hypnosis is not a "state" or "trance." Nor does it derive from suggestion. Rather, Barber looks at the interaction between hypnotist and subject. He sees the subject as hopeful and expectant about the situation and thus open to the operator leading and structuring the experience for his subject. He calls this "perceptual-cognitive restructuring."

These views, although helpful and important in understanding and researching hypnotic phenomena, offer only partial explanations of hypnosis. The authors agree with Josephine Hilgard, co-researcher and wife of E. Hilgard, when she points to limitations in a "nothing-but" theory of hypnosis. Hypnosis is a complex phenomenon and must be explained by multivaried factors on psychological, physiological, and sociological levels. All the many views of hypnosis can contribute to our understanding and application of hypnosis. (Hilgard, 1970: 249) One must be wary of oversimplification in apparent parsimony: Occam's razor can shave too close.

Shaffer

There are many other hypnotists who have contributed to current understandings in the field. G. Wilson Shaffer has written and worked extensively with hypnosis over many years. Many of his ideas from the 40's and 50's are now being rediscovered. Shaffer and Dorcus pointed out that "mental set" of the subject is important in inducing the more complex phenomena of hypnosis. The subject's past experiences and ideational processes at the moment determine to a certain extent whether the suggestions given will be accepted.

Shaffer believed that hypnosis is always voluntary. The hypnotized subject cannot be forced to do something which conflicts with his values and beliefs. Dorcus and Shaffer believe that the authenticity of hypnosis need not be questioned. However, they felt that hypnosis should be demystified and is most effective when used in combination with other therapies.

Weitzenhoffer

Weitzenhoffer, an important modern theorist, writer, teacher, and researcher, postulated that the difference between hypnotic and waking phenomena are essentially qualitative, not quantitative. He holds that suggestibility is the key factor. He has written several comprehensive books and clinical teaching manuals which carefully spell out mechanisms of suggestion with applications.

Unlike Shaffer, Weitzenhoffer believes that the subject is the passive participant in the hypnotic process and that hypnotic behavior can be called "non voluntary" or "involuntary." He defines hypnosis as:

> "A condition or state of selective hypersuggestibility brought about in an individual subject through the use of certain specific psychological or physical manipulations of the individual by another person (hypnotist)."
>
> (Weitzenhoffer, 1957:32)

This definition applies to self hypnosis since the self takes on both the role of hypnotist and subject.

Indirect Hypnotherapy

Milton Erickson was the founder of the Indirect Method of Hypnosis which draws upon much of the history discussed above, but also has some unique contributions. Erickson developed his views of hypnosis from experiments he did to investigate the nature of hypnosis. His formal research first began during a 1923-24 seminar on hypnosis at the University of Wisconsin under Clark Hull. His first experiment indicated that Hull's strong conviction that the operator of hypnosis controls the subject's experience was not correct. Subjects developed spontaneous trances quite naturally during periods of introspection. He found that suggestions, rather than serving as commands to be followed obediently, constituted "No more than a point of departure for responsive behavior.": (Erickson, 1964: 158)

Erickson experimented on thousands of subjects during his years as a professional. Generally he found that the more simple, permissive, and unobtrusive the technique, the more effective it proved to be both experimentally and therapeutically. Erickson observed that:

> The less the operator does and the more he confidently and expectantly allows the subject to do, the easier and more effectively will the hypnotic state and hypnotic phenomena be elicited in accord with the subject's own capacities and uncolored by efforts to please the operator.

His main conclusion from this research was that the operator is unimportant in determining hypnotic results, regardless of his understandings and intentions.

> It is what the subject does, not the operator's wishes that determine what shall be the hypnotic manifestation.
> (Erickson, 1964: 162)

He recommended that hypnotic research of the future be based on subject evaluations and subject performance rather than on the experimenter's words. This view implies the possibility for self hypnosis.

Numerous volumes have been written about Erickson's approach to hypnotherapy, with new books coming out every year. Some of the most relevant major interpretations will be reviewed.

Erickson and Rossi

Rossi co-authored several books with Erickson. They stated their basic position on hypnotherapy as follows:

> We view hypnotherapy as a process whereby we help people utilize their own mental associations, memories, and life potentials to achieve their own therapeutic goals. Hypnotic suggestion can facilitate the utilization of abilities and potentials that already exist within a person but that remain unused or underdeveloped because of lack of training or understanding. The hypnotherapist carefully explores a patient's individuality to ascertain what life learnings, experiences, and mental skills are available to deal with the problem. The therapist then facilitates an approach to trance experience wherein the patient may utilize these uniquely personal internal responses to achieve therapeutic goals.
>
> (Erickson, Rossi, 1979: 1)

This description draws together the basic ideas in Rossi's earlier work with Erickson.

The goals of therapy are accomplished through a three stage paradigm: preparation, therapeutic trance, and ratification. The first stage involves a period of preparation during which the therapist explores the patient's life experiences and encourages a constructive orientation toward therapeutic change. The second phase, activation and utilization, involves trance. The patient learns to draw from his own mental skills, associations, and trance abilities. Phase three gives the patient an experience of ratification of trance and the therapeutic change which has taken place so that he can begin to integrate his unconscious learnings with his conscious mind. Rossi states that this three-stage paradigm is basic to understanding Erickson's clinical work. Much of the self hypnotic approach which we have developed in this book derives from years of study with Erickson and Rossi. Therefore, we will describe the three stages in detail below.

During the preparatory phase, good rapport is established with the patient. Rapport derives from mutual acceptance, which Rossi (1977) described earlier as "Yes Set." The therapist interviews the patient to ascertain what early learnings and life experiences are available for utilization in therapy to promote health and growth. These may be hobbies, interests, life roles, mental sets, personality characteristics, mechanisms of defense, or perhaps just the presenting problem of behavior. Similar to Jerome D. Frank's theory (1978), the patient has problems because his belief systems and frames of reference are limited, which does not permit him to function well and cope with life circumstances. Hypnotherapeutic preparation introduces new attitudes, belief systems, and expectancies. The stage is set for therapy to take place.

In the next phase, "Therapeutic Trance", the patient is guided into trance. Here, the patient's life skills and learnings are used to bring about the hypnotic experience. The experiential content of therapeutic trance varies with each patient. The sequence of therapeutic processes involves fixation of attention, depotentiating habitual frameworks and belief systems, unconscious search and unconscious processes.

Fixation of attention has been widely employed as a means of induction, both historically and in current literature. Erickson emphasized that fixation need not be on an external object but is better placed upon an object of the individual's own inner experience. Since trance is an inwardly directed state, it is better initiated by directing the client's attention toward his own inner or subjective experience. People are unique individuals as well as sharing a common nature. Standardized methods of fixation frequently do not account for this individuality. What interests and fascinates one person may not interest another. Erickson (1967) believed that too much attention to externals militates against trance induction, while conversely, use of internal, spontaneous imagery can lead to development of hypnotic phenomena such as hallucinations. Simply accepting and focusing the subject's attention on his own experience and behavior can lead to his attention being fixated. The reader will notice that many of the exercises in this book will encourage following one's own inner experiencing, associations, and thoughts. The path of self hypnosis begins within.

When attention is fixated, the usual mental sets and frames of reference may be "depotentiated." (Erickson, Rossi, 1979) This means that the subject's typical conscious patterns of associations can be suspended, or "put in brackets" (Husserl, 1964), allowing new, latent or preconscious patterns of thoughts, feelings, attitudes, and behavior to emerge and become actual.

Creative learning takes place through the mental "gaps" that occur when people's typical patterns of association are broken up:

> A creative moment occurs when a habitual pattern of association is interrupted...the creative moment is thus a gap in one's habitual pattern of awareness. Bartlett (1958) has described how the genesis of original thinking can be understood as the filling in of mental gaps. The new that appears in creative moments is thus the basic unit of original thought and insight as well as personality change.
> (Rossi, 1979:6)

Erickson and Rossi believed that this suspension of unadaptive response systems permits the creation or emergence of new patterns of response essential for health. This position is compatible to that of Kubie who stated:

> The measure of health is flexibility, the freedom to learn through experience, the freedom to change with changing internal and external circumstances...The essence of normality is flexibility in all of these vital ways. The essence of illness is the freezing of behavior into unalterable and insatiable patterns.
> (Kubie, 1975: 21)

In order to attain an open and receptive mental state, the limited perspectives must be set aside. Erickson recognized early in his research that people often have difficulties with this. He discovered that confusion, doubt, overloading, binds, and other such methods tend to bring about an uncertainty or a gap. Rossi described a number of techniques used by Erickson to help clients let go of their rigid sets automatically and naturally in response.

The indirect forms of suggestion help patients bypass their learned limitations so that they are able to accomplish a lot more than they are usually able to do. The indirect forms of suggestion are facilitators of mental associations and unconscious processes.

(Erickson, Rossi, 1979: 7)

The indirect hypnotherapist calls upon a variety of techniques to activate a search within the patient's own repertory of learnings for new responses to his problems. The search appeals to many natural mechanisms of human nature such as curiosity, filling in pauses, response to implication, personalizing a general statement. Metaphors, analogies, puns, and allusions can stimulate new ideas or a changed perspective.

The hypnotic response is the culmination of the cooperative efforts of hypnotist and patient. It is experienced typically as happening by itself. Indeed, the more unconsciously initiated, the more surprising it is. Hypnosis makes possible a wealth of experience which clients can have, such as body experiences (heaviness, lightness, hand levitation), immobility, hallucinations, to name just a few. These unusual experiences can initiate new abilities. The response comes from the subject's own background, life experiences, and genetic endowment, yet it represents a different organization and integration, a new response. Because the response is effortless, the learning can be far more powerful.

Creative personality reconstructions are possible through hypnotherapy. In this approach, troublesome and negative personality traits which tend to remain constant are utilized for therapeutic purposes. Different creative interpretations and frames of reference permit new possibilities to emerge, often surprising to the client. What had seemed to be a negative quality can be transformed into an asset, and the client's self-concept changes to include a new way of thinking about himself. The personality traits can be thought of as elements in the chemical molecule of the personality. In Chemistry, as analogy, there is a difference between a mixture and a compound. The elements or traits can recombine to form a new molecule with new properties or potentials, rather than just resorting.

Erickson and Rossi have based this theory on a fundamental statement made by Erickson in 1967:

> The reality of the deep trance must necessarily be in accord with the fundamental needs and structure of the total personality. Thus, it is that the profoundly neurotic person in the deep trance can, in that situation, be freed from his otherwise overwhelming neurotic behavior, and thereby a foundation laid for his therapeutic reeducation in accord with the fundamental personality. The overlay of neuroticism, however extensive, does not destroy the central core of the personality, though it may disguise and cripple the manifestations of it.
>
> (Erickson, 1967: 13)

Because the central core is basically healthy (the unconscious), indirect hypnotherapy does not need to analyze the neurotic problems. Instead, the therapeutic process frees and strengthens the natural, healthy part of the personality to experience, respond, act, and learn.

In an earlier book, Rossi (1972) conceptualized the unconscious as the source of creativity. He stated that symptoms are the beginnings of positive change. Implicit in Erickson's concept of trance reeducation is that returning the patient to his own natural unconscious functioning restores him to the wellsprings of his personality.

Hypnotherapy initiates a small change in the symptoms, behaviors or attitudes. This tends to gain momentum and start other changes through the system or structure of the neurosis, when enhanced by the therapist. (Erickson, 1979) Small changes can be such qualities as the intensity, the duration, the frequency, the initiating stimulus of the symptom, or many other possibilities. Incorporating the patient's world of meanings helps to make the small changes relevant and helpful in altering the patient's difficulty.

Many people do not recognize when they are in a trance since the unconscious is activated and the conscious mind is dissociated. Trance ratification can be a powerful indicator to the subject that something important has taken place. Ideomotor phenomena can act as a trance ratifier for the patient to experience. This helps confirm the learnings which have taken place in trance and acts as an integrative process. Ideomotor, ideo-sensory, and other phenomena also may link thought and action, often metaphorically symbolizing the natural ease with which the patient may find himself automatically behaving differently. This tends to confirm to the subject that he has indeed experienced something different which he comes to recognize as trance.

Erickson and Rossi developed the many subtle intricacies of indirect suggestion and its applications for many psychological disorders. What is illustrated over and over again is the rich potential of the trance state to give the subject new experiences of himself and throw doubt on the usual perspectives. This guides the patient to reinterpret himself and his difficulties so that the problem either dissolves or can be resolved. The patient finds new strengths, strategies, and renewed hope.

Jay Haley

Jay Haley developed many of his concepts of strategic family therapy from studies he did with Erickson. Throughout his studies and in his books on Erickson, Haley emphasized the communication theory which he developed earlier with Bateson. His interpretations of Erickson's work emphasize certain qualities and do emphasize others.

In 1952 Haley and his associates applied the theory of logical types (Whitehead, Russell) to psychotherapy and communication theory (Sluzki and Ransom, 1976). The thesis of this theory is that there is a discontinuity between a class and its members. The class cannot be a member of itself nor can a member be the class, since the class is at a different level of abstraction, a different logical type. This led to the discovery that learning is not a single level phenomenon, but that a person also learns to learn. Paradox can arise out of this. The classic example is from Epimenides: "I am lying." Is he telling the truth?

> This paradox can occur because a negative statement classifying another negative statement occurs in a single message so that the class and its member are self-referent and the discontinuity between the two classes is breached.
>
> (Sluzki and Ransom, 1976: 60)

Bateson applied the theory of logical types to communication. He saw man as a classifying being who is labeling the communicative messages he emits, generating paradoxes at times. A message which qualifies another message at another level of abstraction was called a meta-message. Metacommunications are at a higher level of abstraction and are thus communicated implicitly.

Another concept they developed was framing. Framing is exemplified by the logical paradox:

(All statements written within this frame are untrue)

In communications, one person indicates with a framing message how subsequent messages are to be received.

> The fuller description included the idea that when one person communicates two levels of message to another when these levels both qualify and conflict with each other, the other person is faced with an impossible situation. He cannot respond to either level without violating a prohibition at the other level, so he is wrong whatever he does. The bind becomes complete when the "victim" cannot leave the field or comment upon his impossible situation.
>
> (Sluzki and Ransom, 1976: 68)

Haley (1963, 1967, 1972) viewed Erickson as a master of strategy. Haley compared Erickson's hypnotherapy to the process of therapy itself. In trance induction the subject is directed to go into trance and exhibit phenomena which are supposed to be involuntary, e.g. in a hand levitation the hand raises seemingly by itself. The subject does not feel as if he controls this movement at all. There is a paradox here, according to Haley, since the hypnotist is imposing incongruent directives: the subject has voluntarily come for hypnosis and thus does not want to leave the field. Yet, the options are contradictory; to follow the hypnotist's directive to act spontaneously. This is the classic double bind situation.

Haley compared this to most forms of psychotherapy. For example, in psychoanalysis the patient is directed to spontaneously free associate. Generally, the patient does certain things which he is directed to do as part of therapy, yet the changes which occur happen not directly from the voluntary acts but somehow spontaneously occur when the time is right.

Erickson developed methods for dealing with resistance which Haley considered one of the cornerstones of his approach. It is the job of the therapist, according to Haley, to somehow maneuver the patient to alter his symptomatic patterns. Erickson would encourage resistance. Thus, if the patient had a headache, Erickson would focus on the need for the headache. Haley (1973: 24) saw this as a maneuver to get control:

> The subject is thereby caught in a situation where his resistance is defined as cooperative behavior. He finds himself following the hypnotist's directives no matter what he does, because what he does is defined as cooperative.

This is an example of utilization. Whatever the client presents, Erickson accepts and uses, altering it ever so slightly to bring about the beginnings of change. Erickson uses the analogy of the course of a river:

> If he opposes the river by trying to block it, the river will merely go over and around him. But if he accepts the river and diverts it in a new direction, the force of the river will cut a new channel.
> (Haley, 1973: 25)

The reader may wonder how these concepts of strategic interventions from the operator can possibly be relevant to self hypnosis. Applications can be made in terms of the attitude one takes toward oneself in working with self hypnosis. One of the major points of the Erickson approach is not to fight your nature but to learn to work with it. In the exercises which follow we show the reader how to become aware of the response and to follow it. In this way, change evolves naturally and effectively.

Self Hypnosis Today

The evolution of hypnosis has been sketched from its early historical roots, when practitioners had to fight for the right to even practice hypnosis, to modern hypnosis which has developed into an accepted discipline. Self hypnosis has also grown in its acceptance and has many practitioners today who have written about their approaches. Each one draws upon one or more of the theories of hypnosis which we have described in the history, usually taking their view for granted as the best definition of hypnosis. This tends to delimit what techniques follow.

Many varied aspects of hypnosis are included in this book, presenting a broad spectrum of techniques. The reader can experiment and discover which approaches come most naturally to him with his own individuality. He can then explore new possibilities and learn to master what was difficult or even impossible at first.

Chapter 2
Suggestion: Direct, Indirect, and Beyond

In this sense autohypnosis becomes a means of extending or broadening the range of human experience. It becomes a means of exploring and maximizing human potentialities. This exploration can be enhanced by an attitude of expectation and respect for the potentials of the unconscious and the new modes of functioning that can be gained. Consciousness can never be certain of what is going to be experienced, but it can learn to interact constructively with whatever altered mode of functioning the unconscious makes available.

(Erickson & Rossi, Vol I, 1980; 132)

Suggestion: 1) the process through which an idea is brought to the mind because of its connection or association with an idea already in mind. 2) in psychology, the inducing of an idea, decision, etc. by means of a verbal or other stimulus, in another individual who accepts it uncritically, as in hypnosis.

(Webster's New World Dictionary, 1964)

Suggestion, as implied in the dictionary definition, is more concerned with process than the content of ideas. Often, people attempt to use self suggestion with too much emphasis on the content of what they wish to suggest. The conscious, rather than the unconscious is activated to accomplish this, which could obstruct effective therapy. Suggestion can activate unconscious processes that vary with the individuality of the client and his or her needs. Analytical work sometimes overemphasizes the content and its historical causal explanation. Through suggestion one can get in direct contact with the inner processes to encourage and bring about change, whether directly or indirectly.

Direct and indirect suggestion are important tools in self hypnosis. If principles are carefully abstracted from theory, a series of fascinating experiments become possible in which to explore and develop one's responsiveness to suggestion, as well as trance potentials. This can be useful for self-directed change. The conscious mind need not and indeed should not dominate the unconscious and impose ideas upon it to be helpful. There are a number of ways in which the conscious and unconscious can interrelate to make creative adjustment possible. Suggestion uses the links between psychological and physiological levels. This chapter will delineate the mechanisms of suggestion and different types of suggestion. Exercises in suggestion will help the reader to familiarize himself with his own suggestibility which can be especially useful when combined with trance.

Relaxation and stress reduction can be brought about by suggestion to help heal many chronic conditions such as ulcers, high blood pressure, back problems from tension, and so on. It can be interesting and fun to experiment with different phenomena and experiences. Abilities that are developed become useful skills to enlist for accomplishing valued goals.

When psychogenically based symptoms subside, meanings and symbolically bound conflicts may become available to work through. Conflicts that are unnecessary to work on will not be troublesome: inner wisdom guides the process.

There is a belief held by some that symptom relief will cause other symptoms to be substituted in the psychic economy. The logic of this position is based in the conservation laws of mechanical forces: energy bound in neurotic symptoms must be expressed somehow or else the conflict may erupt; they believe symptoms serve to stabilize the personality. The empirical world does not support this: most experts agree that probably about 80% of headaches are psychogenic, neuromuscular in origin, from tension. Yet, rarely does the use of aspirin to relieve headaches bring instability and disorder. Indeed, psychiatric conditions are often first worked with by medication and then psychotherapeutically. Excessive discomfort distracts from therapy. Intense anxiety may militate against therapy. Depression can prevent a serious attempt to change.

Many conditions are helped when symptoms subside. Jerome D. Frank pointed out the great value of experiences of mastery in recovery from mental distress. They give the client hope that he can alter his condition and boost his self esteem. (Frank, 1971)

Symptoms that do not subside with proper treatment probably indicate that deeper disturbances do need to be corrected. Symptoms may serve as an inner alarm signal to pay attention and do something to change things.

Suggestion can be used for self help and as part of a therapeutic process. Understanding suggestion requires recognition of the subtleties of conscious and unconscious process. Experiment with the ideas and exercises presented in order to personally experience how to use suggestion for oneself. Hypnotic theory has a different meaning when it is personally experienced. Unlike other disciplines, hypnosis and suggestion are more understandable when felt.

The main emphasis of this book is self hypnosis. Therefore, we deal primarily with auto-suggestion, that is suggestions which are given to oneself.

The whole process of auto-suggestion, according to Coué, consists of the acceptance of an idea and its translation into a reality. Both of these operations are performed out of awareness, by the unconscious mind. It makes no difference whether the original idea comes from within the individual or from outside by another. "In both cases it undergoes the same process: it is submitted to the unconscious, accepted or rejected, and so either realized or ignored." (Brooks, 1922: 55) Circumstances sometimes suggest depressing thoughts and feelings, or at other times, happy and positive emotions. Thus, to Coué, auto-suggestion is the basis for suggestion's effects, even those which come from another person. Ultimately the suggestion must go through an acceptance by the individual, even if this occurs without his awareness.

Spontaneous and Induced Suggestion

Coué made a distinction between "spontaneous" and "induced" suggestions. Spontaneous suggestions are the occasional, everyday, involuntary experiences of responding to a stimulus as a suggestion, without intending to deliberately. Induced suggestion occurs when the individual deliberately sets himself to have an experience to accomplish a selected goal using the techniques of suggestion. The suggestions to be given, he believed, should be permissively general and positive.

Exercise

Most people have had a time in their life when they sat around a camp fire, watching the dancing flames and listening with ever increasing fascination to a terrifying tale of ghosts and spirits. Later, as you ventured back to your sleeping quarters, sounds had an eerie tone, shadows appeared to move inexplicably, and an overall feeling of fear was experienced. In this example, an idea and fantasy presented to you became a reality for you: you felt as if you were in the midst of apparitions, even if only for a few moments. As another instance, think of a time when you might have been feeling a bit depressed. You meet up with a good friend whose pleasant smile and cheery disposition seems to magically lift you from your doldrums. In her presence your own thoughts and feelings seem unnecessarily glum, and you are released from your negative mood.

You may think of your own examples, which can illustrate principles of waking suggestion. Suggestion is a natural part of our daily experience. Most people simply do not know how to use it in a positive way.

Exercise in Spontaneous Suggestion

Learning to be aware of spontaneous suggestion can be as helpful as working with the more well-known, induced type. First, cultivate awareness of these occurrences, noting and observing patterns of natural, spontaneous suggestion as they occur. Concentrate on the experience as you notice it happening. This requires careful observation. Learn to recognize the sensory or intellectual modalities that are typically suggestive to you. As you become more aware of them, you will learn more about yourself. For example, the sounds of someone in the kitchen can suggest dinner or perhaps awakening in the morning. The smell of food can suggest its taste and the experience of eating as well as hunger. People with a cigarette habit often find that the smell of cigarette smoke suggests to them that they have a cigarette. Later, if they successfully give up the habit, this is no longer suggested. If an experience of disgust has been evoked, they might instead think of it as disgusting, and feel nauseous. Watching an exciting football game, there are involuntary movements in involved spectators, as if dodging, running, or catching the ball. There are many other ways of responding to spontaneous suggestion; the individual variations are important in understanding one's own patterns of response. It is easier to pass from this understanding to more complex suggestive links.

A sensation can give rise to a suggestion by interacting with an idea that was apriori. When we are expecting someone to come visiting, a hamster playing in its cage may seem to sound to us like a knock on the door. A telephone may be heard to ring when the house is essentially silent, if the imagination is active enough. The ideas and expectations bring about a spontaneous suggestion. We interpret events and sensations partly according to expectancies. Spontaneously, experiences, ideas, and emotions may all be suggested. The overeater unintentionally may have eating suggested by certain cues such as anger or frustration. Eating behavior is not, in this instance, a simple response to hunger. There is no normally rational connection between eating and anger.

Coué believed the thoughts we think can bring about experiences from the unconscious by means of acceptation or being accepted which transforms them automatically into reality. Induced auto-suggestion simply implies directing this entirely natural process, so that the mechanisms of mind tend to bring the suggestion about. This is strongest when the conscious tides of the mind are lowest and unconscious association is most likely to flow. Jung believed that the threshold between conscious and unconscious lowers at times, allowing concentration to take place effortlessly and attention to be focused through involuntary processes, brought about by the imagination. At such times, induced suggestion can be very effective. In Coué's conception there is no difference in effect between hetero and auto-suggestion since it matters not whether the idea is presented by one's own conscious mind, by circumstances, or by another person. Once the unconscious accepts the idea it tends to be brought about. Coué believed that imagination is stronger than will. Suggestion stimulates imagination. The walls of will and resistance can thus be overcome.

Suggestion as Focused Attention

Braid considered concentration of attention to be essential for successful hypnosis and a prerequisite for the acceptance of suggestions. By narrowing the attention, suggestions which are presented to the mind are met with little or no competition. This approach to suggestion tends to view hypnosis as a state of focused attention which greatly facilitates suggestibility.

Exercise in Fixation of Attention

If you would like to experiment with this, find an experience available to you with the natural quality of fascination, such as a fireplace fire, a peaceful full moon over a lake, or some other visually stimulating scene. Let your attention focus or be drawn exclusively to it. Ensure that you can be undisturbed as you watch, relax, and permit your thoughts to dwell on nothing but the fire, moon, or whatever you have chosen to use. In time you may have an experience of drifting into a state of deep absorption. At this point you can experiment with self-suggestion, inviting such phenomena as relaxation of your arms and legs, and perhaps all your muscles. You might suggest heaviness, lightness, warmth in arms or legs, coolness in forehead and so on. Each successful experience tends to reinforce the general tendency of responsiveness. When you have had enough of this, you will feel yourself beginning to orient towards the awake and alert state. You may want to give yourself a suggestion to awaken. Experiment to see what works best. Many like to stretch, tighten and clench, and then relax their hands at the end.

Another classic exercise in fixation involves looking upward until your eyes become tired, then giving yourself the suggestion that your eyes will become heavy and want to close. Often the eyes water as they begin to close. Wait for your response. Follow and appreciate the individuality you might manifest in the situation: you can learn about yourself and your tendencies in this way. If you find yourself unable to open your eyes, you have gotten in touch with the involuntary nature of response to suggestion. Some find this easier than others to bring about. With a further suggestion you can release your eyelid muscles from this, such as "Soon I will once again be able to open my eyes." Rest a moment, then begin to stretch and reorient to the conscious state.

Suggestion as Ideomotor Phenomena

Bernheim, who historically was the popularizer of hypnosis as suggestion (See Chapter I), saw suggestion somewhat differently from the fixation or auto-suggestion theories. His view of suggestion involved ideomotor action. The idea which is suggested to and received by the mind tends to realize itself automatically in action through the ideomotor effect. There are many mind-body interactions which occur automatically and can be used to bring about changes. (See Chapter 4 for details and exercises on the ideomotor effect)

Exercise

Close your eyes and think about a tart lemon. Imagine this as vividly as possible. If you have salivated, you have experienced the effects of a suggestion automatically taking place through ideomotor action.

Expectancy as a Factor in Suggestion

An important factor affecting whether a suggestion is accepted or rejected involves the mental set of the person at the time the suggestion occurs. "Positive thinkers", a school of practical, applied philosophy in the late 1800's and early 1900's conceptualized that the positive or negative atmosphere created by one's characteristic "set" and thoughts about the world create a tendency for personal destiny to evolve in a positive or negative way. This has led to some useful understandings about life. If one expects the worst to happen, one may paradoxically tend to bring it about through unconscious ideomotoric mechanisms, which then confirms the belief. Therapy entails altering expectations in a positive direction so that favorable expectations towards the future are developed. (Frank, 1973) A basic theme of these positive theorists is to attempt the transcendence of normal, average functioning to reach unrealized potentials. With a positive set, adverse circumstances can become a challenging invitation to grow as a person and to transcend the narrow boundaries of adjustment that might prevent a troubled individual from overcoming difficulties. Negative expectancies can lead to the person's disregarding the potential invitation, or else to experience it as an invitation to suffer the symptoms and be diminished, often feeling discouraged from tackling challenges wholeheartedly. Direct suggestion aims at the conscious facets of these expectancies, to turn them around.

Suggestion in Context

Weitzenhoffer (1957) notes the importance of suggestion within the total situation. He emphasized that suggestion takes effect within the context, the "suggestion situation." The person giving the suggestion, the person receiving the suggestion, and the circumstances at the time are part of this. The effect or response to a suggestion is a part of this complex unity. Responses to ideas that are intended as suggestions are modified by many factors. Suggestion evokes changes in the subject which do not engage voluntary participation.

Kretch and Crutchfield (1948) think that suggestibility is mostly a function of the individual's psychological field. This position is similar in noting the importance of the setting or circumstances. Lack of structurization in the surroundings is an important factor in the acceptance of suggestion. If the situation or circumstance has some ambiguity in meaningfulness, the person is unable to respond with the full use of his or her rational faculties. Groping about for cues takes place. In this state of indecision and frustration there is a tendency to be especially susceptible to suggestion. Further, the complexity and difficulty of a situation adds to the influence of suggestion. Simple, clear circumstances can be understood and reacted to rationally. As there are increases in difficulty, the individual may fail to understand things and consequently must react to the problems presented with whatever suggestive assistance he can draw upon. The ambiguity leads the person to lower defenses and scan for some guidelines or parameters to help interpret matters.

Coué took a strong stand in favor of self-suggestion:

> Of all the questions which arise, the most urgent from the viewpoint of the average man seems to be this—is a suggester necessary? Must one submit oneself to the influence of some other person, or can one in the privacy of one's own chamber exercise with equal success this potent instrument of health? Induced auto-suggestion is not dependent upon the mediation of another person. We practice it for ourselves without others being even aware of what we are doing, and without devoting to it more than a few minutes of each day.
> (Coué, 1923: 42)

Coué wanted to liberate from what he feared as a potential dependency on others. This was a primitive conception of hypnosis as it has evolved today. Many modern approaches are client-centered and non-dominant in their orientation.

Further Differentiation of Suggestion: Direct, Indirect, Efferent, Afferent, Immediate, Mediate

Sidis (1898) was one of the first theorists to clearly specify a distinction between direct and indirect suggestion. Direct suggestion occurs when a hypnotist tells the subject exactly what he is to experience and the subject experiences this. For example, the hypnotist might say to the subject that he will feel warm, or become very tired, or upon awakening he will hear a knock at the door. Rossi states a similar conception: "Direct suggestion, by contrast, presents subjects with a stimulus that identifies what the results should be." (Erickson, Rossi, Rossi, 1976: 268)

Suggestions can also be given in a subtle manner. Sidis points out that nonverbal communication is suggestive in an indirect way.

Suggestion: Direct, Indirect, and Beyond

> Instead of openly telling the subject what he should do, the experimenter produces some object or makes a movement, a gesture, which in their own silent fashion tell the subject what to do.
>
> (Sidis, 1898: 19)

He further distinguishes between what he calls the "afferent" and the "efferent" side of suggestion:

> ...in suggestion, we deal, on the one hand, with the impression of the suggested idea on the mind and its acceptance by consciousness; this is the afferent, sensory side of suggestion; and, on the other hand, with the realization of the accepted idea; this is the efferent, motor side of suggestion.
>
> (Sidis, 1898: 21)

Direct and indirect suggestion represent the afferent, or sensory receptive side of suggestion. The process of actually carrying out the suggestion through some physiological effect, the efferent side, Sidis classified as immediate or mediate.

> In short, when there is a full and complete realization of the idea or order suggested, directly or indirectly, we have that kind of suggestion which I designate as immediate...Instead, however, of immediately taking the hint and fully carrying it into execution, the subject may realize something else, either what is closely allied with the idea suggested or what is connected with it by association or contiguity.
>
> (Sidis, 1898: 22)

Thus, the subject may not exactly obey the suggestion given but will carry out something similar. For example, the hypnotist might suggest that upon awakening the subject will pick up a book from the table. Instead, the subject takes the pencil sitting nearby. This is like responding to the suggestion as an open-ended suggestion, which permits the creative utilization of the individuality of the subject. Erickson and Rossi define it in terms of the subject's consciousness. They view the indirect suggestion as defined by how the subject experiences the response. It takes place without the subject's conscious awareness of how or why. During direct suggestion the subject has some sense of the relation between suggestion and response. When indirect suggestion takes place the subject is usually surprised. (Erickson, Rossi, Rossi, 1976: 268-9)

These subdivisions help to clarify the complexity of factors involved in therapeutic self hypnosis. Throughout the chapters of this book the reader will experiment with many forms of suggestion. Some might find that they respond best to the direct approach while others may prefer a more subtle indirect method. Experiment and think about what happens. What works best for you? Be sensitive to mediate affects as well as the more obvious immediate ones. Accept what your individuality gives you. Hypnotic learning takes place in the mind of the subject. Associations to the suggested idea can be just as helpful as immediate response to the suggestion. Observe and note your own reactions and tendencies. With time and insight you will know and be able to predict your responses.

Indirect Suggestion

Erickson and Rossi have clearly delineated many of the parameters of indirect suggestion in a number of volumes. (1976, 1979, 1980) A basic theme is to bypass the conscious mind in order to mobilize and activate latent potential from the unconscious. Coué used the conscious mind to activate unconscious potentials through the imagination. The Nancy School emphasized the automatic reflex ideomotor response to bring about changes. Braid and the British theorists utilized the focusing of attention to enhance suggestive responsiveness. Erickson creatively enlisted these and many other natural mechanisms of the unconscious, trusting that it would find its own way to free the individual from his problematic difficulty or discover new, creative ways of coping.

Erickson and Rossi consider the unconscious to be intelligent, creative, healthy, and free. Education in unconscious functioning involves response to indirect suggestion. People can outgrow their problems, utilizing their own repertoire of learnings and capacities that they do not even know they have. Trance returns the individual to the natural state as a foundation from which, unhampered by conscious limitations, new potentials in behaviors, thoughts, and attitudes are created.

Indirect Forms of Suggestion

There are many forms of indirect suggestion well described by Erickson and Rossi. (1976, 1979) Some of them can be creatively adapted to self hypnosis. Open-ended suggestions, compound and contingent suggestions, acceptance set, and binds (to name a few) can be adapted to self hypnosis. Simple exercises in each will be given below, but more complex applications must wait until the reader has tried trance, since indirect suggestion involves unconscious processing.

> In general, indirect forms of suggestion utilize the subject's tendency to mediate or actually construct his own hypnotic responses out of the stimuli and suggestions preferred by the operator.
> (Erickson, Rossi, 1980: 454)

This concept can be applied in self hypnosis as one develops an open attitude towards the inner self. Using indirect suggestion in self hypnosis requires that the subject sets the stage for himself with the general concept of the suggestion and also suggests that his unconscious can create both the specifics of the suggestion and the response, both outside of conscious awareness.

Open-ended suggestions work well for self hypnosis. Conscious self suggestion can also use these, but not as effectively as in trance. When the unconscious is dominant during trance, the open-ended suggestions are guided by the unconscious, inner needs. The indirect approach teaches one to appreciate this, that by trusting the unconscious to be positive, a therapeutic process can take place by which the personality gradually becomes more positive and a self actualization mechanism tends to guide therapy.

The self actualization process is similar to Gestalt Therapy's organismic self-regulating mechanism. In therapy there are "inner signals" that the client must be attuned to, to pay attention and do something about, gradually leading towards homeostasis, the natural balancing tendencies towards health and maturity. By resolving or coming to terms with the important, central concerns, people are freed to make their lives more satisfying and meaningful. The inner signals guide this process: tensions, discomforts, as well as comfortable feelings. In self hypnosis the meaning of the inner signals is not always clear but they do guide the individual towards health and maturation intuitively.

Indirect Associative Focusing

If associations are permitted to wander aimlessly, they will not simply wander into empty space, dissociating without direction. Conscious and unconscious patterns naturally tend to dominate and direct the flow of associations. Flows of associations can be used to help link up with unconscious patterns of therapeutic importance that may affect or even restrict the unconscious to redundant patterns. Through contemplating and meditating on many associated meanings and experiences, one can learn to get in touch with and elicit certain wished-for responses, without manipulating oneself mechanically like a puppet with techniques. In the process, one "warms up" or prepares for the next phenomenon or experience. J.L. Moreno conceptualized all life as continuously going through a warming-up process, by which each experience "warms up" for the next. Making actual the imagined, vaguely energized meanings, attitudes, ideas, and experiences is the general direction that indirect associative focusing brings about. Some may find it similar to meditation. Cognitive, perceptual, or experiential environment makes it more likely that a certain response will occur. Natural reflexes and intuitions can guide the exploration of meaningful

Suggestion: Direct, Indirect, and Beyond

patterns of ideas, feelings, and attitudes. These meanderings may be very productive.

Through imagination, focusing on the ideas and associations gradually mobilizes expectancies in the muscles or sets that are laden with meaning. When explored in trance with indirect associative focusing, these become resources that are available. Contact with these inner wellsprings of the personality, encoded in memory, attitudes, and sensory-emotional complexes helps bring about the desired change.

Acceptance Set

A basic technique in indirect suggestion, the acceptance set, can also be adapted to self hypnosis. In heterohypnosis, the hypnotist establishes a genuine rapport, a feeling in the client of being understood by listening and enlarging upon the client's concerns and perspectives. Similarly, self hypnosis is facilitated by developing a genuine "mutual" inner dialogue with one's own unconscious. (More on this in Chapter 6)

Compound and Contingent Suggestions

In their simplest form, compound suggestions are made up of two statements connected by "and". (Erickson, Rossi, Rossi, 1976) For an example of this, hold your arm out and see how tired it gets.

Exercise

Contingent suggestions involve two usually unrelated suggestions which you relate together, one dependent on the other, for the purposes of an hypnotic experience. Experiment with the example to hold your arm out and suggest, "As I hold my arm out it becomes heavier and heavier." Alternatively, hold your arm out and suggest, "As I let myself relax my arm becomes lighter and lighter." Notice the differences between the two. In these examples a contingent link between holding out the arm and a suggested effect is made.

Binds

Bind suggestions are numerous and potentially complex in their nature. Erickson and Rossi (1976, 1979, 1980) offer many complex varieties of binds, double binds, reverse set double binds, etc., which are effective in heterohypnosis. For the purposes of self hypnosis some binds can be used while others are difficult to perform on oneself. The following bind exercise can be helpful in learning to apply binds with oneself.

Exercise

Sit comfortably and place your hands on your lap. Pay careful attention to your right hand, then your left hand, and ask which one will become lighter or heavier. Wait for a response and wonder which one will do what.

Posthypnotic Suggestion

Suggestion can also be applied posthypnotically, which means it is to take effect after the trance is terminated. Posthypnotic suggestion is a field of application that derives naturally from trancework, allowing unconscious factors to take effect. Erickson and Erickson (1941) in an interesting study of this phenomenon, noted that posthypnotic suggestion tends to induce a trance when it takes effect. Their definition is most useful:

> A posthypnotic act has been found to be one performed by the hypnotic subject after awakening from a trance, in response to suggestions given during the

trance state, with the execution of the act marked by an absence of any demonstrable conscious awareness in the subject of the underlying cause and motive for his act.

(Erickson and Rossi, 1980: 388)

The posthypnotic act spontaneously induces a brief trance, linked to the performance of the act. When responding posthypnotically, a trance can be easily evoked. Posthypnotic behavior can be used in self hypnosis to enhance trance learnings. There may be various factors that can affect this phenomenon, as described below. As always, experiment to discover the most effective ways for you to respond. It is probably best to start with a simple posthypnotic suggestion that permits time and individualization of response. This can be encouraged through open-ended suggestions, permissive and vague. Many varieties of posthypnotic suggestions can be applied, which tend to enhance rapport, leading to a better relationship with the unconscious mind. As response to one posthypnotic suggestion is gained, try several suggestions in succession. Ease of hypnotisation, deeper relaxation, and other responses can be suggested or visualized as taking place posthypnotically.

Suggestibility and Hypnotic Susceptibility

An old, time-honored dispute in psychology is that between nature and nurture. This applies to susceptibility and suggestibility. Some believe that susceptibility and suggestibility are determined by genetic factors, that a person is born a suggestible type. Others hold that nurture is more primary, that people can learn to become more responsive to suggestion and to hypnosis through practice and experience. Still others hold that it is a combination of the two, with an individual balance between them. The authors have found that people have certain talents, perhaps one is more visually oriented whereas another is kinaesthetic. Natural abilities can be used as starting points for new learnings and possibilities.

There are many differences in experimental findings concerning suggestibility and hypnotizability. Research has not always confirmed with certainty what are the definitive traits of suggestibility or hypnotizability. ("The Problem of Hypnotizability, A Review", 1963). Certain factors are generally accepted as indicative of high hypnotizability. High scores on the Stanford Hypnotic Scales of Hilgard have been widely used to define this, assuming constancy. High scorers are characterized as capable of being highly involved, imaginative, adventuresome, and spontaneous, which Josephine Hilgard has described as healthy personality traits. Diamond (1974) holds that hypnotizability is not a constant, but rather appears to be a learnable skill that can be enhanced. In exploratory self hypnosis or clinical hypnotherapy, scales of susceptibility might be used to help as maps and guides in locating talents and deficits in hypnotic functioning, rather than to set limits that become the parameters of abilities. Erickson's indicator was response attentiveness. In self hypnosis, the task and at times, the challenge, is to develop your capacities further, through careful, sensitive, creative exploration, which can be fun. (Erickson & Rossi, Vol. I, 1980: 143)

Erickson explained in an early paper (Erickson, 1952)

> "Personal experience extending over 35 years with well over 3500 hypnotic subjects has been most convincing of the importance of subject individuality and time values. One of the author's most capable subjects required less than 30 seconds to develop his first profound trance, with subsequent equally rapid and consistently reliable hypnotic behavior. A second remarkably competent subject required 300 hours of systematic labor before a trance was even induced; thereafter, a 20-30 minute period of trance induction was requisite to secure valid hypnotic behavior."

Creative artistry in communication and technique, coupled with sincere rapport with inner nature and needs, leads to response to suggestion. No factor or condition need ultimately determine the response of the subject in self hypnosis: if the willingness and motivation to experiment are present, one can develop and evolve an ability to respond unless there is a good reason inwardly not to. If you suspect this is the case, you should not attempt to force matters. Develop and use your unconscious intelligence. Ideomotor questioning can help discover answers when carefully and sensitively applied. Sometimes, professional support helps in problem solving and therapeutic changes that may be necessary. At other times, self support may be adequate.

Chapter 3
The Unconscious

Like the empty sky it has no boundaries
Yet it is right in this place, ever profound and clear
When you seek to know it, you cannot see it
You cannot take hold of it

But you cannot lose it
In not being able to get it you get it
When you are silent, it speaks

When you speak, it is silent
The great gate is wide open to bestow alms
And no crowd is blocking the way.
(Watts, 1957:145)

Unconscious Intelligenoc

The unconscious involves aspects of human processing which lie outside of awareness. The unconscious has its own intelligence and a logic which, though apart from the rational, can take in information, think, and draw conclusions. Whereas the conscious mind uses logical reasoning, the unconscious functions by inner preconceptual processing. It does not follow sequential logic. Milton Erickson used the example of solving a problem. Consciously one might reason from A to B to C to D. The unconscious mind may backtrack D to C to B to A in order to figure out how the answer was found. People do not experience the processing itself, but do perceive the product of the unconscious thinking as intuitive insights.

The unconscious is not confined to conflicts repressed by the conscious mind, as some analytical models contend. Nor is it simply primitive primary processing. The unconscious can involve conflicts and include primary processing in an effort to reach for higher integration but there is a sophistication and intelligence to the unconscious which is individualized and oriented. Rather than merely being the repository of the negative, the unconscious is the reservoir of potential. This chapter unfolds many facets of the unconscious in an effort to help familiarize and sensitize to the subtle unconscious indicators which will become the building blocks of self hypnotic skills.

Everyday, Out of Awareness Phenomena

The unconscious is continually active during everyday life. For example, as the reader sees the words on the page, he is probably not aware of his foot. But now that "foot" is mentioned he might notice that it is cold or heavy or tingling. As the attention is turned there, the foot experience can be perceived. The experience in the foot was always present, but when thoughts were directed elsewhere these feelings were unconscious. Attention mediates perception of this experience, but the experience exists whether perceived consciously or not. The issue of unconscious perception is similar to the old philosophical question: if a tree falls in a forest and no one is there to hear it, does it make a sound? People have unconscious experiences and thoughts about problems, life experiences, etc. of which they are not aware. This does not mean that these experiences do not occur since they can be recalled at a relevant later date.

The unconscious registers a multitude of experiences at once. Information processors believe that the mind can hold 5 plus or minus 2 bits of information at one time. (Miller) Anything beyond this goes unnoticed consciously but is taken in unconsciously. The unconscious continually absorbs much more information than the conscious mind perceives at any given moment. This kind of data is used when a witness to a crime is hypnotized to recall details of the event. The witness feels unable to remember certain specifics, such as a license number, but under hypnosis the entire scene is recreated as a vivid hallucination. The witness can search through his image to see the license number as if watching a movie replay. The information was taken in initially, outside of awareness, and stored unconsciously.

The unconscious is the reservoir of the thoughts, memories, and learnings which one experiences over the years. As a child grows he learns not only how to walk, read, write, etc., but also how to learn. With each stage of development certain skills and abilities are mastered. This requires various applications of intelligence, emotional maturity and body co-ordination. Abilities are stored in the unconscious, not just as the manifested skill which was learned, but also as a more generalizable potential to learn how to learn. For example, the skills used in forming letters are taken for granted in adulthood, yet those same abilities, to make lines, circles, spacings, might be applied later as an architect or in work as an artist or in the construction fields. These skills can be automatically applied by the unconscious. For example, a writer focuses on the ideas he is trying to express. The forming of each letter on the page takes place without thought, regulated by the unconscious.

The unconscious holds many learnings and understandings which are applied in different contexts throughout life. Connections can be made without conscious effort in trance, as will be shown.

Automatic Habits

Much of the daily routine is automatic, regulated by the unconscious. The alarm goes off in the morning and it is unpremeditatively shut off. People walk so naturally and easily that they never think about the complex links between mind and body which are coordinated unconsciously. In trying to remember yesterday's activities, some parts are murky and difficult to recall. But after concentration more and more details can be reclaimed bringing automatic activities into awareness. Not all unconscious activity is inaccessible to consciousness, as in this case.

Lawrence Kubie stated:

> Once any such act is fully learned, it can be initiated quite independently of inner physical prodding merely by contemplating the goal. As this happens the entire constellation is triggered as a unit by the symbol which represents the goal; and we thereupon become unaware of the innumerable intermediate steps which make up the act...It is in this way that our thinking processes acquire the ability to leap over many intervening steps as we perform complex authentic processes. Moreover, this is the root of intuitive thinking, whether in science or arts.
> (Kubie, 1961: 33)

The Unconscious as Set: Russian Set Theory

The Russians theory of "set" offers an alternative to the psychoanalytic "dynamic" unconscious. This "set" theory is helpful in our understandings of the unconscious.

Psychoanalyst Bellak distinguishes three levels of the unconscious: 1) the physiological, 2) the structural, 3) the dynamic (Bassin, 1969) The physiological and structural levels are:

> The noncognized somatic processes not reflected in consciousness either directly or on the basis of symbolization...the structural aspects of the unconscious represent the noncognizance of the automated actions and the neural activities on which the formation of any content of consciousness depends, activity which creates these contents but remains imperceptible after its task is accomplished, for example, early memories of learning to walk.
> (Bassin, 1969: 410)

The Unconscious

The physiological and structural levels are not the content of psychoanalysis. Level three, the dynamic aspect, is unawareness which results from repressed psychological content, unacceptable to consciousness but occasionally struggling to awareness. The psychoanalysts ignore the first levels of the unconscious and concentrate only on the third. The Russian findings about the unconscious indicate that the first two levels hold the source for understanding how the unconscious functions. The approach to self hypnosis developed here draws on all three levels, finding a great deal of useful understandings from the first two.

In 1860 Fechner did research showing that an illusion of the estimation of weight could be produced from a preliminary repeated raising of objects of the same size and weight. When an experimental object which was the same size but different weight was presented, subjects reported it to be as heavy as the preliminary weights. He explained this phenomenon as "motor set". Later, Uznadze developed experiments which expanded the earlier hypothesis. He found that the illusion created in the early motor set experiments was based on a far more integral and deep-seated condition than motor phenomena. His research tested the same principles using alternatives to motor response such as pressure response, visual response, and auditory response.

Uznadze concluded from all these experiments that the early theory of motor set was too limited. The phenomena of set involve modification of the individual as a whole which expresses itself in a wide variety of perceptual modes. He theorized that during the control tests, a specific state (set) is developed and fixed. Even though the set is not a content of consciousness, it is responsible for the course of the process of consciousness. He specified two levels of mental life.

1. The level of the sl (setting level) is where behavior is completely conditioned. These sets control behavior and impulses out of awareness. 2. The level of objectification occurs when man perceives something through his objectification of it rather than reacting to the thing itself. Russian theorists developed this into an alternative approach to the unconscious. Complex stimuli act upon people as signals, eliciting reactions outside of awareness. This separation

between the objective effect of a stimulus on the one hand and consciousness of the stimulation on the other is called dissociation. (Bassin, 1969)

Dissociation occurs often in life and accounts for the automatization of habits, where something which begins under conscious control gradually loses its conscious character. Walking, writing, or driving a car are all examples of processes which began with deliberate effort and attention and become automatic after time and practice. The Russians believed that all voluntary actions have periods of being unconscious.

Uznadze's theory of set provides a model for understanding the complex noncognized influences which act upon a person outside of his awareness. These influences have significant effects upon the dynamics of succeeding conscious experience.

Erickson and Rossi developed the concept of the Acceptance Set or Yes Set as a way to engage cooperation and receptivity to hypnosis and suggestions. They found that when the hypnotist tried to relate to the subject through his real interests and concerns the subject developed a positive feeling of involvement and acceptance of the process. This led to an easier transition into trance. They called this "Acceptance Set". (Erickson & Rossi, 1976: 58)

Trance as Unconscious Functioning

> The centipede was happy, quite
> Until a toad in fun
> Said, "Pray, which leg goes after which?"
> This worked his mind to such a pitch
> He lay distracted in a ditch
> Considering how to run.
>
> (Watts, 1957:27)

The trance is a state where the unconscious processing flows freely with little or no interference from the conscious mind. The indirect forms of suggestions help to "depotentiate" or disengage the conscious mind thereby allowing the unconscious to think, problem solve, and/or experience.

Unconscious thinking tends to be without an object or content of consciousness. Edmund Husserl, in his phenomenological philosophy talked of consciousness always comprising an intention or meaning complex for all possible processes of consciousness. (Zaner, 135) However, therapeutic unconscious processing has been described by Rossi as a gap, or creative moment, in the stream of consciousness. It is a point when the everyday learnings, meanings, interpretations, and beliefs are temporarily suspended and the individual can experience anew.

The unconscious is capable of functioning without any one set of fixed assumptions, beliefs, logic, or meaning sense. There can be freedom from the bonds of preconception, a chance to make new connections and original thought leading to new conclusions. Erickson and Rossi used the therapeutic trance to bring about this natural ability of the mind. A healthy adjustment can be built upon the foundation of this kind of functioning in which the limitations and unhealthy experiences are bypassed. Kubie believed that preconscious systems of processing are the source of creativity. The unconscious includes these characteristics as part of its capacity.

Associative Qualities of the Unconscious

The unconscious thinks in a stream of associations. It has been described as a free flow of natural, active creative processing without intervention of conscious purpose. The associative principles were widely studied in the late 1800's and early 1900's. William James carefully defined and described it. The unconscious makes associations just outside of awareness throughout our day. This process is extremely useful in hypnosis and trance processes. James believed that the basis for the law of association is:

> When two elementary brain processes have been active together or in immediate succession, one of

> them, on reoccurring, ends to propagate its excitement into the other.
>
> (James, 1898: 566)

James describes "impartial reintegration" as the process whereby an event or experience can spark a run of associations, link detail to detail in a backwards chronology. All ideas are equally weighted. This kind of association is rare because certain thoughts usually predominate over the rest. The predominant items are those which appeal most to our interests. (James, 1898: 572) Only when the interest is equally diffused over all the parts, does this law not hold.

> Our musings pursue an erratic course, swerving continually into some new direction traced by the shifting play of interest as it ever falls on some partial item in each complex representation that is evoked. Thus it so often comes about that we find ourselves thinking at two nearly adjacent moments of things separated by the whole diameter of space and time. Not till we carefully recall each step of our cogitation do we see how naturally we came by Hodgson's law to pass from one to the other...this is the ordinary process of the association of ideas as it spontaneously goes on in average minds. We may call it ordinary, or mixed association.
>
> (James, 1898: 573)

Some associative processes are influenced by habit. For example, if we mention the word swallow, an ornithologist will think of birds, a throat specialist will think of throat diseases, a person who is thirsty might realize how much he wants a drink of water. Other factors influencing associations are recency of the experience, vividness of the original experience, and congruity in emotional tone between the reproduced ideas and moods.

Association by similarity occurs from the free flow of associations, where similar types of associations become linked to form compounds which can link to each other. Thus, seemingly dissimilar ideas can end up mentally connected.

James further points out a difference between the train of association and the movement of thought. All in all, the process of association is complex and multi-faceted. Research is difficult since the phenomenon is outside of awareness.

However, the flow of unconscious associations is not random but evolves out of one's individuality. It reflects one's past, likes and dislikes, and conflicts, potentials and expectancies, as well as many other external and internal stimuli that can be crystalized in associative metaphors.

In the therapeutic trance, learning takes place. Sometimes the learning is an original discovery. Other times it is a reassimilation, recombination, or restructuring of old experiences. New possibilities and changes follow from recombination and interspersal of new ideas into the associative processes of the unconscious mind.

Dreams: Free Flow of Images

Unconscious processing has been described thus far as thoughts. But sometimes the unconscious is manifested as images or pictures. These images often reflect deep levels of inner experience which are not consciously known. A single picture can contain many possible meanings and learnings. Dreams are like this, where a very few images can symbolize a wealth of meanings. In trance, dreams can occur spontaneously and yet meaningfully. For example, a client in hypnotherapy had a vivid image in trance of a woman in a dark shawl. Upon awakening she described the experience and felt that it was puzzling. Therapeutic exploration brought out the connection to her Italian background and her feelings about her mother who had been sedentary and withdrawn. This client was involved in many community organizations, having decided early in her life to be different from her mother. The image brought forth associations which helped her to better understand her tendency to over-commit herself.

Sometimes dream images are misleading. One client had a recurring dream of a frightening monster chasing her. Night after night she was repeatedly terrified by the image. She was a very quiet, sweet girl who always tried to be considerate, kind and warm. She rarely got angry and found such emotions difficult to handle. As she worked in therapy she began to sense that the monster was not a foreign body attacking her, but rather was her own angry feelings crystallized into one image. As she accepted this she was able to include more of her personality into her everyday life and stopped having the nightmares. The unconscious can express a complex emotional conflict in one seemingly terrifying image. However, this unconscious image, though feared and avoided, turned out to hold the key to resolving the difficulty.

Dreams have also inspired great discovery. Kekule's discovery of the benzene ring structure emerged from a dream. He had been struggling to uncover a structure which could account for the unique properties of benzene. One night he fell asleep working on his calculations. He had a very unusual dream. He saw a snake twirling around and around, chasing its own tail. Eventually the spinning snake caught its tail and turned as a circle. When Kekule awoke, he knew that he had solved the problem. Benzene was a ring, a possibility he had overlooked! He went back to the data and was able to empirically show the validity of this discovery which is still considered correct today. His unconscious synthesized the intellectual understandings into a symbol which he consciously traced back to the data.

Prince viewed dreams as one of many altered states in which people work out difficulties unconsciously. He states:

> Under conditions of stress, individuals have resorted to a repertoire of automatic self-healing mechanisms. The most important of these so-called altered states of consciousness—dreams, dissociated states, a variety of religious experiences.
> (Zeig, 1982: 383)

This approach to dreams is used in our approach to self hypnosis where the dream symbolically expresses or represents a concern. If worked with properly in trance one can utilize this valuable communication from the unconscious to resolve difficulties and expand potential. Research has shown that hypnotic dreams are similar to natural dreams in regard to character, and so one can work with both in self hypnosis.

Unconscious Expressed Through the Body

The unconscious also expresses itself through sensations and images of the body. For example, during a trance, tingling in the finger tips can lead to a lightness in the hand which develops into an arm levitation. The ability to allow the arm to raise can be a significant unconscious learning in and of itself. For example, one client learned to do arm levitation without any conscious awareness of doing the levitation. She was an extremely shy, fearful, and dependent individual who found that through trance, not only did she experience temporary relief from her discomforts, but also could move freely and unpremeditatively. Levitation taught her experientially to express herself without conscious censor. She gradually integrated this learning into her life by developing her own independence. She never put this experience into words, nor did she ever make a conscious link. She found that her range of options and abilities expanded and evolved naturally. She enjoyed trusting her unconscious to help her; she was often surprised at her own abilities that emerged.

Trance allows many body sensations to occur spontaneously: warming, cooling, lightness, heaviness, floating, movement, catelepsy, etc. The gap between mind and body is bridged through trance and the ideomotor phenomenon which are developed in depth in Chapter 4. The unconscious as it is expressed through the body is an extremely important and useful facet of trance work.

Unconscious as Intuition

Intuition is the language of the unconscious. Jung characterized it as the psychological function which transmits perceptions in an unconscious way. (Berne, 1977: 4) This processing is intelligent and has even been construed as the inroad to truth and higher consciousness.

Aristotle first thought of intuitive functioning as an extremely sophisticated process. He believed that "intuitive induction" is based on the ability of the organism first to experience sense perception, at a higher level of organization to retain sense perception, and at a still higher level to systematize such memories. This implies that intuition can intelligently synthesize data. Since this occurs outside of awareness, the individual knows something without knowing how he knows it. The synthetic processing of the unconscious occurs without a rational sense of how it happens.

> To the rationally minded, mental processes of the intuitive appear to work backward. His conclusions are reached before the premises.
> (Berne, 1977: 149)

People often experience their intuition as hunches, spontaneous familiarity or realizations. Intuitive truth is usually recognized, not learned. Most people are aware of having an intuition and some rely on it. It may be extremely clear for some people and vague to others. Intuition involves a sensitivity to phenomena which are nonverbal and nonrational. Some see this sensitivity as a more accurate way of knowing the truth about reality. Self hypnosis calls forth the use of mental faculties which occur outside of rational knowing. Trance relies upon these non-rational, intuitive modes of functioning through which the therapeutic work takes place.

The Necessity for Both Conscious & Unconscious

Whether intuition is more perceptive than rational awareness is not the issue here. Both the conscious mind, through awareness and rationality, and the unconscious mind, through intuition and unconscious experiencing, are important in development of the self. Jung saw this when he said:

> Conscious and unconscious do not make a whole when one of them is suppressed and injured by the other. If they must contend, let it at least be a fair fight with equal rights on both sides. Both are aspects of life...It is the old game of hammer and anvil: between them the patient iron is forged into an indestructible whole, an individual.
> (Jung, 1981: 283)

The Unconscious as Right Brain— An Oversimplification

In recent years the unconscious has been defined as the right brain. This theory simplifies the conception of the unconscious and of hemisphericity. However, split brain theory is important in understanding the unconscious.

History of Hemisphericity Research

When the brain is looked at under a microscope, the two halves appear to be structured much the same. It is not surprising that through most of history, researchers thought the two halves of the brain functioned identically. It is only in the past 100 years that the very different functions of the two hemispheres have been discovered. Neurologists first realized the left brain controls the right side of the body and the right brain controls the left. However, in the early years researchers evaluated the left side which seemed to control language and complex cognitive abilities as the most important side. According to Gardner:

> The left hemisphere became the one to have, if you are having only one. Indeed, neurologists were fond of citing case reports of individuals who were born without a right hemisphere, or who had lost their entire right hemisphere in an accident or through surgery, who none-the-less coped successfully with the business of living.
> (Gardner, 1976: 353)

Evidence gradually emerged to indicate that the right hemisphere might be important as well. Research in England during World War II revealed that right hemisphere damaged patients were deficient in their ability to organize spatially. (Gardner, 1976) They had trouble finding their way back to their rooms on the wards and even found dressing a problem. Such research revealed that the right hemisphere also played an important part in human functioning such as with basic visual skills, depth perception, gestalt formation, and tactile or somato-sensory skills.

In the early 1960's the two halves of the brain were actually severed. This opened up a wealth of specific understandings. The first split experiment was done on a cat by Ronald Meyers and Roger Sperry at the University of Chicago in the early 1950's. Sperry found that:

> Each hemisphere...has its own...private sensations, thoughts and ideas, all of which are cut off from the corresponding experiences in the opposite hemisphere. Each left and right hemisphere has its own private chain of memories and learning experiences that are inaccessible to recall by the other hemisphere. In many respects each disconnected hemisphere appears to have a separate 'mind of its own'.
> (Gazzaniga, 1973)

Even though the left hemisphere controls language, the right hemisphere could be taught to communicate its rich life by using special techniques. They found that the right hemisphere has some language, can initiate response, can emote, learn, and remember without the left hemisphere knowing.

Although the left hemisphere was superior in managing verbal processing of information, the right hemisphere proved superior in managing visual-spatial tasks. (Gazzaniga, 1973)

More detailed research has determined that both hemispheres process language but that they accomplish it differently, verbally versus spatially. The left hemisphere sequentially transforms each letter into an internal acoustic code (i.e. names them) The right hemisphere examines all the letters simultaneously looking for variations in shape. The left is interested in semantic similarity; the right is interested in structural similarities. (Nebes, 1977) The right hemisphere organizes and processes data in terms of complex wholes, perceiving the total rather than the parts. The left hemisphere analyzes input sequentially. It abstracts out the relevant details and associates these with verbal signals. Drawings by left hemisphere damaged patients had a correct overall configuration but no detail. Right hemisphere damaged patients did drawings full of details but with no coherent organization.

Modern Concept of the Right Brain as Unconscious

Contemporary popularized characterizations of the two brains have gone through a reverse of the old prejudice against the left brain. Now the left brain is considered slow and ineffectual for certain applications: "The classic left-brain approach to dancing is a perfect example of doing something the hard way with appalling results." (Blakeslee, 1983: 23) Blakeslee in his book on the right brain defined intuition as a thinking process which cannot be verbally explained, taking in large masses of data in parallel without separately considering each factor. This he considers to be clearly referring to right brain functions. (Blakeslee, 1983: 25) He goes on to equate the unconscious with the right brain because:

> What makes the unconscious mind unconscious is the fact that, though it influences our behavior, we have difficulty in verbally explaining its actions.
> (Blakeslee, 1983: 26)

The nonverbal memory of the right brain is not accessible to the verbal left brain, just as intuitive unconscious understandings can influence behavior without conscious awareness. From this viewpoint, the individual has two minds—two personalities which can be reacting very differently to the same situation.

Beyond Specialization

These concepts are based on early and incomplete findings of split brain researchers that the right brain was nonverbal and therefore not capable of conscious thought. Brain researchers Gazzaniga and LeDoux point directly to this issue in a later book. (1978) They tested individuals whose two brain halves were severed. They found the right brain subject to be fully capable of answering questions which related to his personal identity, his plans for the future, his likes and dislikes, etc. The authors concluded:

> Thus it would appear that the right hemisphere, along with but independent of the left, can possess conscious properties following brain bisection. In other words, the mechanisms of human consciousness can be split and doubled by split-brain surgery.
> (Gazzaniga, 1978: 145)

The authors' research corroborated with this in that right hemisphere-oriented people were not found to be more unconsciously oriented in hypnotherapy than left hemisphere oriented people. The lefts did better with hypnosis than the rights which seemed at first to contradict the popular right brain theorists. These findings revealed the complexity and variability of human processing. To categorize unconscious as simply nonverbal right hemisphere is to do a disservice to the integrative capacities of the whole person. Gazzaniga and LeDoux feel that specialization theory fails to account for analysis and synthesis which are integral facets of the cognitive repertoire of both cerebral hemispheres in man.

The brain halves can function independently or together. The integration of conscious and unconscious is the basis for working with self hypnosis as presented in this book. Just as an unconscious thought cannot be known without becoming conscious, so many conscious thoughts and experiences are enhanced and colored by the unconscious set, mood, preconception etc. The taken-for-granted assumptive level of functioning will be brought out next.

Context, Environment, and Culture as Unconscious

Assumptive World

Everyone has a set of somewhat implicit assumptions which assist in organizing one's work and sense of self. People predict and anticipate events using assumptions. Jerome D. Frank describes his concept of the assumptive world as:

> A shorthand expression for a highly structured, complex, interacting set of values, expectations, and images of oneself and others, which guide and in turn are guided by a person's perceptions and behavior and which are closely related to his emotional states and his feelings of well-being...The more enduring assumptions become organized into attitudes with cognitive, affective, and behavioral components.
> (Frank, 1974: 27)

Some assumptions are held unconsciously and taken-for-granted outside of awareness. Attitudes which derive from these assumptions often remain relatively stable and can actually influence one's interactions with the environment.

For example, negative attitudes associated with a sense of uncertainty or catastrophic expectations can result in anxiety, discouragement, and an inability to handle certain stressful situations due to past experiences. Attitudes may also be associated with positive expectancies to help people meet difficult circumstances hopefully and confidently. Some attitudes are learned from the interpersonal world of parents, culture, schooling, and friends often without conscious evaluation. Others evolve from the intrapersonal, the interaction of one's own personality with the world. For example, most people think about and carefully choose a profession, but attitudes toward work are often unconscious. Some people implicitly believe that work is a struggle or an uncomfortable ordeal. Others see it as a means to enjoyable free time, something to get through with as little effort as possible. Still others treat work as devotion, the essential meaning in life. These attitudes may have evolved from the parent's way of dealing with work, a devastating social circumstance like the Great Depression, or possibly even from one's own inner dynamics. Whatever the origins, assumptions influence the kinds of real life choices a person makes.

Lebenswelt

Another perspective on the implicit assumptive level of functioning is given by the "Lebenswelt" of phenomenologist Edmund Husserl. He defined the Lebenswelt as the work of common experience upon which all of science and idealized truths are based. People are concerned with one mode or another: animals, things, fellow man. This is pregiven within the individual's context. Gurwitsch, a Husserlian scholar states:

> If the world is always there as pre-given, if living means living in the world, it is because the world announces itself along with the appearance of every particular mundane existent with which we might be dealing. The inexplicit and inarticulate awareness of

the world pervades all our activities and enters into them as their most general, though unformulated, "premise" or "presupposition". Correspondingly, the world, silently accepted as a matter of course, proves to be the ground upon which we pursue all our activities, whatever their orientation.

(Gurwitsch, 1966: 419)

The Lebenswelt is relative to a certain society at a given moment, including the current cultural mores, interpretations, and philosophies. It is the grounds for the existence which is accepted as a matter of course. The life-world evolves, develops, and changes as the community interacts with it through creations, both material and mental. All of this is unconsciously experienced and reacted to, influencing the course of life and development.

Language as Expression of the Unconscious

One arena for the expression of the assumptive world is language. The taken-for-granted perspectives of the life-world are expressed in daily references. Language symbolizes interpretations of reality. Burke states that, whether he realizes it or not, man is a symbol-using animal. He states:

But can we bring ourselves to realize just what that formula implies, just how overwhelmingly much of what we mean by 'reality' has been built up for us through nothing but our symbol systems?

(Burke, 1969: 5)

Language is a way of separating the verbal from the nonverbal, of simplifying the multiplicity which is reality. We mistake the symbolizations for the reality.

Language referring to the realm of the nonverbal is necessarily talk about things in terms of what they are not—and in this sense we start out beset by

> paradox. Such language is but a set of labels, signs for helping us find our way about...such terms are sheer emptiness, as compared with the substance of the thing they name.
>
> (Burke, 1969)

The unconscious is what lies behind and beyond the verbalizations; the rich and varied nonverbal experiencing. Language can express the unconscious when one speaks spontaneously without thinking. The flow of verbalizations, if listened to carefully, can reveal social attitudes, cultural bias, and historical context as well as personal feelings, moods, and inner dynamics. The unconscious is expressed through the use of language and through the spaces between the words, the reality behind the symbol.

B. L. Whorf crystallized this conception of language in general:

> Every language contains terms that have come to attain cosmic scope of reference, that crystallize in themselves the basic postulates of an unformulated philosophy, in which is couched the thoughts of a people, a culture, a civilization, even of an era.
>
> (Carroll, 1956:61)

These terms are taken-for-granted assumptions which help to shape the person in his culture and historical context. Words like "byte" may seem strange to persons unfamiliar with computers, yet the children of the 80's take computer words for granted as part of their understood reality. Similarly, the parents of these children have accepted television concepts like "channels" as part of reality whereas to their parents it was new and extraordinary at first.

Summary

The unconscious is a complex of experiences, events, attitudes, feelings, surroundings, culture upbringing, learnings, and habits which occur outside our awareness of

The Unconscious

them. It includes the everyday taken-for-granted realm of life, the repressed experiences and reactions from the past, as well as little-understood potentials for creativity and surpassing of learned limitations. Once we familiarize ourselves with the multifaceted unconscious, we can begin to make these unconscious potentials useful. How to harness these potentials to accomplish goals will be developed throughout the remaining chapters of this book.

Chapter 4
Mind & Body

> I am my body only in so far as for me the body
> is an essentially mysterious type of reality,
> irreducible to those determinate formulae
> (no matter how interestingly complex they
> might be) to which it would be reducible
> if it could be considered merely as an object.
> (Gabriel Marcel, 1969)

In the early philosophers mind and body were seen as separate. Descarte's famous declaration in the Meditations, "I think, therefore I am" set mind beyond body, and philosophers have had to answer to Descartes ever since.

Cartesian philosophy was based on the theory of knowledge that one can know with certainty only one's own mind; in order to question, to doubt, one must first think, and thus exist. There must be a thinker. "Cogito, ergo sum." The world of objects and of other people can only be proved to exist from the prior existence of consciousness of them. This introduced the notion that reality is dualism: mind vs. body, or spirit vs. matter. Mind cannot be understood as existing in physical space: it cannot be seen, measured or touched, except indirectly or by inference. Only the body exists in space, is measurable, and can be observed directly. Later discoveries would call into question the dualistic view of mind and body.

The Personal Equation

At the Greenwich Observatory in 1796 a seemingly innocuous event took place that was to change the history of astronomy and philosophical thought. Its significance went unrecognized for 25 years. The "Astronomer Royal" of the observatory, Maskelyne, fired his assistant Kinnebrook because his measurements of the movements of stars were .8 per second slower than his own. The method of measurement was usually considered to be accurate to .1 per second. The observer was to watch and time the star's motion from one parallel sighting wire to another in the telescope as a clock ticked. He thought his assistant indolent and mistaken for recording such inaccurate measurements.

Twenty-five years later an astronomer named Bessel noted this. He was so puzzled that he sent for the complete report to investigate whether this personal difference held constant with experienced observers. Together with another astronomer he found that reports differed by more than a full second! The formula they worked out for the difference came to be called "The Personal Equation". Bessel believed that the delay was due to the time that mental processes take.

Later investigators developed and elaborated these findings. In 1850 Helmholtz had claimed that impulses travel slower than sound waves. Later experiments using different methods found variability in the results. Reaction times to measurement efforts also vary with the set or expectation of the observer. Expectant attitudes predispose an observer to react slower or faster, depending on how the expectancies are sequenced.

J. C. Whitehorn, Johns Hopkins Hospital researcher and psychiatrist 1930's-60's, researched whether tall people take longer for the standardized medical knee jerk reflex than short people. Many people had believed that the speed of transmission of nerve impulses was determined by variables such as height or size. Whitehorn found no standardized significant difference, only individual differences. People's reactions are not determined in standardized ways, even though there are many common features. He believed the personal equation was an individual one, not determined by genetic factors.

Fechner was versatile: a humanist, a poet, a physicist and a philosopher with a mystical feeling about the unity of all life with the spirit. He believed plants were conscious and that the whole earth was alive as a unified spiritual being. He wanted to unify mind and body through an equation. He postulated that "The relative increases of bodily energy and measure of the increase of the corresponding mental intensity could be mathematically computed as a ratio between the two." (Boring, 1950: 280) Fechner is known scientifically for psychophysics, which he explained in his text, the *Elemente der Psychophysik*. He stated that the book was "the exact science of the fundamental relations or relations of dependency between mind and body." (Boring, 1950: 281)

Expectancy or set theory was an important force in psychology for many years. As mentioned before, Fechner demonstrated that muscles can be given a set which then persists in experiencing and judging how heavy something is. Fechner showed that after an expectation that a weight of a certain size looks a certain way is given to the muscles, another weight which looks identical will usually be estimated to weigh the same, even though in actuality it is heavier or lighter. Russian psychologists went farther. They discovered that sets or expectations can be given in all of the possible modalities. (See Chapter III for details.)

Expectancy and the Mind-Body Interaction

Expectation and set links the mind and body, as placebo research has shown. Placebos are inert substances which contain no active ingredients of any kind. In early studies subjects thought the placebos contained medicines which would help their condition. They improved and researchers began to suspect that the positive expectation of help did influence the physiological condition toward health. They went even further, conducting experiments utilizing "pure" placebo response. In one experiment (Park and Covi, 1965 in Frank, 1978) the subjects were told that the substance they were being given was a placebo, that it was completely inert, but that many had been helped with placebos and that the experimenter believed it would help the subject. One subject dropped out due to spouse ridicule of the experiment and thus her data was lost. Many participating subjects gained dramatic relief from their problems. All the rest were improved. Some even requested refills.

The influence of the imagination over the body can overshadow powerful medications. In one study, subjects were given a medication that is a powerful stimulant in warm milk. Subjects were told that the warm milk was soothing and usually produced sleep: it did!

These experiments illustrated that there is a powerful interaction between mind and body. How this occurs is not clearly understood, but the mental effect on the body must be recognized and can be used in treatment. The mind need not always dominate the body to be helpful, like the old saying, "The power of the mind over the body," or even, "Mind over matter". There are, however, times when mind directing physiological responses can be very useful. For example, a relaxation and stress reduction response deliberately cultivated can help to heal an ulcer condition. A calm, relaxed response has been used to help lower blood pressure. Research using biofeedback, relaxation training, and other treatments has indicated there is reason to accept that this can be accomplished.

Stress Theory

Stress theory conceptualizes that the attempt to balance or restore equilibrium is primary for the survival of the organism. Selye's stress theory holds that it is just as stressful to experience pleasure or enjoyment ("eustress") as to experience displeasure ("distress") (Selye, 1974) since the organism's inner balance is disturbed. Both negative and positive experiences can be stressors. Every tension relieved is a debit from the checkbook of resources. Rest or change of situation must be used as a credit, to balance the debits, or else eventually the individual is overdrawn and suffers physical symptoms. These can lead to diseases such as ulcers, back problems, high blood pressure and so on.

In Selye's later theory he conceded that stressors can be specific, not merely non-specific. The original stress concept presumed a non-specific, general adaptational syndrome which leads to the difficulty. Personality factors can affect how people experience and handle stress: whether it is experienced as overwhelming and threatening or as challenge and opportunity. As Whitehorn often said, people need challenge. Without challenge, growth and development might never take place. Whitehorn also pointed out that paradoxically, some illnesses are cured by stress, as a symposium on stress had concluded: not all stress is bad for the organism.

Hinkle (1967) reported increases in respiratory illness at crucial stressful points in a person's life. Theorists have studied and correlated stressful changes in the social environment with illness and dysfunction. Smale (1968) reported that serious illness often follows separation of some kind. Supportive therapeutic interaction can help in coping with such life events, enhancing a positive, hopeful response. Support may come from friends and co-workers, intimate relationships, or family as well. All of us have been helped and reassured at times by others during stress. This is one of the values of supportive counselling interactions. What the research indicates is that this kind of help tends to stimulate feelings of hope, raising morale to help meet the difficulties. (Frank, 1973)

> That the relation of people to their society and to the people around them can influence the incidence, the prevalence, the course and the mortality of diseases seems clear enough. The questions at issue are the questions of when they do so, under what circumstances, by what mechanisms, and to what extent.
> (Hinkle, 1973: 47)

Lazarus points out that adaptation to stress includes the psychological interpretation given to the events or stimuli, and that successful coping strategies can modify whether the situation or stimulus becomes helpful or noxious to the individual. (Lazarus, p. 23, in Lipowski, Lipsitt, & Whygrow, 1977)

Frank states that "The most frequent symptoms of patients in psychotherapy, anxiety and depression, are direct expressions of demoralization." (Frank, 1974: 271) Frank shows in many articles and books, the importance of hope: "Efforts to heighten the patient's positive expectations may be as genuinely therapeutic as free association or habit training." (Frank, 1965: 385)

Herbert Benson (1979) illustrated the effects of negative attitudes in the extreme case of voodoo death. He describes documented instances of voodoo death as a real phenomenon, mediated by attitudes of hopelessness and certainty that escape is impossible. Residents of certain islands such as Haiti, Jamaica, or even the Bahamas may have heard or seen instances of voodoo curses, after which dire consequences followed for the recipient. A shared assumptive world of beliefs and attitudes about the power of voodoo contributes to its devastating effects. Locals know curse symbols. When a curse is made, there is a fertile ground for the mechanism of self suggestion to bring about the feared event.

Curt Richter, of Johns Hopkins, experimentally induced sudden death in rats by drowning them. Rats immersed in protective jars lasted as long as eighty-one hours before death. Rats given an experience that it was hopeless to escape held firmly in the experimenter's hand, died in as short a time as one to fifteen minutes. Rats raised in company with other rats handled the stressful situation far better, surviving longer than rats reared in isolation. (Benson, 1979)

The common point in these findings on stress is that body and mind interrelate. Sometimes body experiences and sensations can communicate what is important and urgent; at other times they can be background to what is demanded in a real life situation. How can thoughts and experiences that seem to be "in the mind" be brought to the level of "the body"? How can the mind-body gap be bridged, when it is there? Stress which is seemingly physical can be thought through as problems to be solved, and coped with better. Conversely, mental disturbances can be affected by concentration to relax the body. In both cases, stress can become a challenge to meet and overcome.

Gestalt Therapy: A Theory of Mind-Body Unity

Gestalt Therapy, founded by Frederick Perls, addressed the mind-body split as an instance of defensive alienation. Mind and body interrelate as a unity which he called a "Gestalt". The mind is experienced as embodied in each individual's unique organism which is also in relationship to the environment. The point of contact and natural identification is the boundary where activity or interaction takes place. When tension and consequent interruption takes place, either through deliberate or neurotic obstruction, people tend to identify themselves with one part and alienate themselves from the other. Which area they choose depends on their interest or need, as well as the sense of identity of that individual and the situation he or she is in. If you are sitting in class, for example, you probably will tend to be more identified with your mind, thoughts, abstractions, and so on. Your body concerns are background unless an urgent need or interest begins to draw your attention and involvement. If you are attempting to study and a throbbing headache comes on, it tends to draw your attention away from the material, until you manage to either take care of whatever you need or else perhaps stoically accept it or relax it away. Suddenly body awareness and identification with that becomes foreground or primary. The awareness of body sensations is part of the signalling system the organism has to take care of needs and concerns. This can start the motor of action to do something about the needs or tensions. By getting in touch with discomforts, tensions, and consequent needs, healthy and motivated, creative adjustment can naturally be started.

At other times it becomes useful for the purpose of one's values or identifications, to alienate or dissociate body concern temporarily from awareness in order to accomplish goals. For example, in an important soccer match, the San Diego "Sockers" had a number of injured players vital to the team. They gave themselves over 100 percent to the team effort in the final game in order to try to win the 1986 MISL Championship. Their identity with the team and the goal of winning was most important to them. Body concern over pain and discomfort became background, whereas the tension and commitment to win was primary. Players temporarily surpassed the limitations posed by their injuries.

Body experience in Gestalt Therapy is one of the primary experiences of Being-in-the-World, for as Perls would have said, "I am my body". A body technique originally from early Gestalt *(Ego, Hunger, & Aggression)*, was characteristically used to get in touch, to be aware, and cure oneself of neurosis. The client was to concentrate on body sensations and "take responsibility" for any experienced tensions. The reader can experiment with this in the following exercise.

Body Focusing

First describe to yourself what you are experiencing. Then, change the descriptive, inner dialogue sentences that one thinks from e.g. "There is tension in my back", to "My back is tense", to "I am tensing my back", and pay close attention to the sensations there. Wait for a phantasy or train of thoughts, feelings, and ideas associated with it. For example, an image might appear of being in a tense and difficult social situation, handling it with restraint in spite of feeling annoyed. Intuitions and ideas about what things mean usually pop into your mind when you open it attentively. With practice, you learn to note and observe carefully whatever emerges or manifests itself.

This exercise illustrates the close interrelationship which Perls felt existed between the mind, expressed through thoughts, feelings, and even language, and the body. Conversely, the body speaks a sort of language through gestures, posture, and movements which the mind can use as a language to decode emotions and experiences that are unconscious. In Gestalt Therapy, the therapist observes the body languge of a patient while he sits and talks. Then the therapist interrupts the patient's verbalizing or "bullshit", as Perls referred to it, and requests the patient express what his posture or gesture really intends. The body does not lie, as Perls would say. Through "getting in touch" or rather, by expressing the meaning that the patient infers is being indicated by his or her gesture or posture during discussion of his problems, the patient learns to expand his perception of himself, to learn more about his deeper feelings, attitudes, thoughts, and so on, which helps to resolve his conflicts.

Perls had a balance theory of adjustment based in the physiological theory of homeostasis. Homeostasis is the tendency of the body to seek equilibrium, balance, and rest. He postulated that this holds for the personality as well as the body. The personality goes into a tension state when a need emerges and becomes urgent. The need automatically tends to organize behavior to satisfy it. Thus, if a person needs some water, he begins to feel thirsty and notice potential sources of water. Thoughts and impulses that are oriented around water and drinking tend to occur to the thirsty person until he or she has some liquid. This resolves the tension and brings completion to the unity of pattern, which Perls termed the "Gestalt". The organism then returns to a neutral balance state of "creative indifference". (Perls, 1969) A new need eventually organizes a new gestalt, beginning the process again. People can get in touch with what they really need through feeling and becoming conscious of their impulses, phantasies, tensions and discomforts. Body sensations and perceptions can thereby assist in getting in touch with what is needed or important.

The person discovers that there is wisdom already present. To the Gestalt therapist, body and mind are an integrated unity in health. Duality or split between mind and body indicates problems. Attempts to deliberately control the self are basically neurotic. The organism has its own built-in control which tends to balance itself through need-satisfaction and completion of unresolved business. Self regulation is a natural characteristic of life. Body perception is part of self perception. To learn more about oneself involves becoming more sensitive to body experience. These skills are helpful for self hypnosis as well, since the reader will sometimes need to recognize minute cues from the body in working with the hypnotic state. As will be shown later in this chapter, hypnosis works with the mind and body as a unity, where thoughts can be reflected in the body and vice versa.

Exercise in Body Perception

Lie flat on the floor. Draw your knees up so that the soles of your feet are flat on the floor. Let your body relax, and release all unnecessary tensions. As you permit your attention to wander about and scan your body, certain tensions in certain areas may become more evident, while other areas of your body sensations seem unimportant or less interesting: background phenomena. For example, you might find your back is somewhat tight and uncomfortable, which you had been experiencing earlier but had not really noticed. When you pay attention to it you might find a phantasy or a memory pops into your mind having to do with some thoughts and feelings about annoying situations during the day. Continue to concentrate on whatever spontaneously attracts your attention. This is the essence of awareness technique: blending concentration with what spontaneously attracts your attention. It is easy to go from here to relaxing and suggest that the back tensions could let go (to continue with our example) so that your thoughts could be less distracted from working on the more fundamental concerns. Otherwise you could decide not to fret about it.

Your body can give you a great deal of information through experiencing such things as tensions, comforts and discomforts, various feelings and sensations. There is a subtle art to attuning to this and using it wisely. Einstein is famous for utilizing his body sensations intuitively to help him discover relativity. He believed that relativity existed because of experiences he had in his body. These sensations caused him to work backwards mathematically to prove that these intuitions were true. Jazz musicians such as Miles Davis speak of the use of their bodies to sense new creative patterns. Detectives are able to discover things because they have a "hunch" or feeling about it. These are all examples of body-mind links being used for positive goals.

Sensory Awareness

Sensory awareness as developed by Charles Brooks and Charlotte Selver from the work of Elsa Gindler, approaches mind and body from another angle. Problems in the mind clear up when body awareness is sensitively experienced. Practitioners of this art carefully concentrate on the details of sensory experience. Thoughts become background to this. Focus is given to kinaesthetic sensations such as touch, movement, relaxation, tension, weight, and breathing. Subjects often find their lives markedly enriched and chronic tensions, psychosomatic problems and character disorders eased. Therapy can be facilitated by this means as well. Clients in the course of their therapy learn to experience without interference from thoughts. This can be helpful in the growth process. These skills have a hypnotic quality in the sense of focused attention and facilitation of relaxation. The reader can experiment with an exercise to further enhance sensory awareness. Sensory awareness can be developed in everyday activities. Selver and Brooks often had students experiment with walking, sitting, and even such mundane tasks as washing dishes.

Exercise in Sensory Awareness

In order to develop your awareness of sensations for hypnosis this exercise is best done in the shower or bath. Begin by running the water at your usual temperature. Feel the water as it hits your body. After a few minutes turn the water up to a slightly warmer tem-

perature. Notice how this affects the sensations in your skin, whether your muscles relax, and any other feelings you might have in your body. Next, turn the water down to a cooler temperature and pay attention to these sensations. Compare how you feel now with how you felt when the water was warmer. Do not make the water too hot or too cold for comfort.

Following the shower, dry off. Sit or lie down in a comfortable position. Scan through your body with your attention, without changing anything. Simply notice what you experience. Watch your breathing. Is it easy? Labored? Slow? Quick? After awhile try to relax your breathing. Sometimes you can place your hands lightly on your rib cage and feel the rise and fall of your chest with each breath. In this approach, as in hypnosis, you do not try to deliberately change your breathing; rather, you allow the change to take place naturally. Can you allow your whole ribcage to take part in your breathing? Can you permit your abdomen to relax and move with your breathing? Can you feel your lower back and waist move? Your shoulders?

Body Therapies

The release of body energy is important in many therapies. Bioenergetics, based in the ideas of Wilhelm Reich, later evolved by Alexander Lowen and Stan Keleman held that conflicts a person suffers are expressed symbolically through the body. This shows up as postural problems, chronic tensions, and dissociated experience of the body. Personality types tend to communicate unconscious meanings characteristically through the body. Classically, the hysteric expressed conflicts through the body in such ways as hysterical blindness or paralysis. In these instances the patient feels as if he is unable to see or move, yet there is no physical reason for the problem. Obsessives tend to be more oriented around thinking and do not notice their bodies. Manic-depressives often

Mind & Body

have poorly defined body boundaries. Schizophrenics often do not recognize their body image, or else have fluctuating hallucinatory images of themselves and their bodies.

Body therapies believe that the cure for neurosis is through the body, not the mind. Therapeutic procedures can involve taking on a certain posture which is supposed to help release emotions. Massage which breaks up connective tissue, such as Rolfing, is thought to free locked-away conflicts. The client then has access to the previously repressed emotions and can work on them emotionally, through abreaction, and mentally, through careful analysis.

The body-oriented therapies have shown that there is a close interaction between emotions, thoughts, and the body. Thus, learning to be relaxed and loose can often help with tense attitudes. Focus on the body experience can permit its use as a symbol system to resolve conflicts nonverbally. Hypnosis works with both the mind and body, thereby approaching problems on a number of levels at the same time.

Ideomotor Phenomena: Communication with your Unconscious Mind

Hypnosis has a pragmatic solution to the mind-body split, through ideomotoric phenomena as well as all ideo-dynamic links. This phenomenon occurs naturally when mental thought, image, or experience is automatically translated into a body experience, movement, or sensation. There is no actual separation: thought becomes action, image becomes motoric response, imaginary sensory experience becomes actual sensory phenomena.

In deeper trances, the unconscious reinterprets sensory and motoric phenomena into phantasies, hallucinations, dreams and other symbolic expressions that compound many potential meanings. Careful analysis and study of such phenomena can be very helpful in self therapy.

Erickson and Rossi used ideomotor phenomena in many varieties of techniques as doorways to other phenomena and abilities. An early paper of Erickson's exploring ideomotor phenomena as gateways to trance and suggestion is the "My Friend John Technique". In this multifaceted paper, through anecdotes and theory, Erickson describes how vividly imagined experiences assist people to tap into their own potentials for trance experience. By utilizing the spontaneous talents a person may have to clearly visualize someone else going into trance, a thread is spun which leads to his own trance. This kind of effect is natural and often surprising to the individual. It was implicit in Bernheim's work on the ideomotor phenomena centuries ago.

An everyday example of this is when the symptoms of an illness may be induced in oneself by empathy with others who are ill. A comical example is the classic movie, "The Disorderly Orderly" with Jerry Lewis as a hospital orderly who found himself becoming imaginatively ill with the symptoms of the patients he treated, though he tried not to be influenced.

The simplest way to understand ideomotor phenomena is to experiment with it. The following exercise will give the reader an experiential sense of the conscious-unconscious, mind-body interaction.

Exercise in Ideomotor Effect: Chevreul's Pendulum

Take a plumb bob, easily procured at most hardware stores, or else use a heavy object on a string, like a locket, a ring, or fairly large machine nut. Draw a large pattern on a standard piece of notebook paper, of a cross at right angles. Sit on a chair with both feet flat on the floor. Place the paper on the floor beneath you, as you rest your arm on a table, desk, or on your knee and hold the weighted string over the paper without letting the weight touch the paper. Imagine the weight swinging, picture it vividly, either side to side or front to back. As the pendulum picks up momentum, imagine that the swings get bigger and bigger. Next, picture the pendulum changing direction, or swinging in a circle. Do not force it to move, nor should you will it to swing. *Simply imagine the swinging as vividly as possible, and wait for the response.*

When some try to do this, they find that the movement is very tiny. Others discover that the pendulum seems to "take off" and have a great deal of intensity. With practice the effect evolves; the exaggeration of small movements can be learned. Then, communicating with your unconscious becomes possible. You can ask questions of your inner mind and get 'yes', 'no', or 'maybe' replies, by assigning no to one of the axes on the cross and 'yes' to the other, 'maybe' to circling.

The following exercise is a fun application of the ideomotor effect.

Ideomotor with Paper Match

Take a paper match, split it all the way up almost to the head, so that it looks like the letter A without the crossbar. Straddle a table knife with it, touching only the ends of the match to a table and try to prevent it from walking off the knife. An interesting paradoxical effect ensues. In order to make the match walk in one direction or another, simply confidently imagine it doing so. The match willingly cooperates. Resist or force it and it will change direction rapidly. 'Phantasy is fun,' as the author's first hypnosis teacher G. Wilson Shaffer used to say. Have some fun doing ideomotor and ideosensory exercises, and the rewards are great.

Thoughts, when given more energy, become action as the patterns of activity shift from the phantasy potential level to the actuality level. (Perls, 1967) Freud's early theory of complexes, repressed ideas and impulses in conflict that influenced the neurotic individual may be understood as a logical extension of this view. The energy level tends to determine whether the thoughts remain just thoughts, or become action and whether actions can lead to thoughts. Actors sometimes use this to help kindle an emotion: performing an action associated with an emotion, like an angry gesture, may help to conjure it up. Thoughts and ideas that are highly stimulating emotionally tend to bring about meaningfully linked action. Conversely, a catharsis may take place emotionally from thinking through and visualizing a scene or situation that is personally significant. In a scene from his videotape entitled "Grief and Pseudogrief", Fritz Perls demonstrated that going through grieving and recalling her memories in detail helped to free and release the client to grow and develop as a person, learning that the traumatic experience could be reinterpreted to help her when confronted``.

Ideomotor theory as mentioned before, holds that once an idea is presented to and accepted by the mind, it automatically gets translated through the nervous system into the muscles. This is similar to the theory of induced suggestion which we described in Chapter 2 except that here the nervous system is involved. Ideomotor and ideosensory suggestions can be experienced and explored, to learn to become sensitive to the nuances of the unconscious link between mind and body, especially the involuntary and voluntary systems of movement, sensation, and imagination. These useful skills will be explored and developed in the chapters to follow.

Body Image

Body image is the term which psychologists use to refer to the attitudes, beliefs, and experiences one has about one's body. Body image focus varies symbolically with traits of personality. The extensive research of Fisher (1970) indicated that certain character traits are associated with certain patterns of focus of attention. There are also characteristic distortions of perception of one's own body that are associated in general with specific emotions and attitudes. Thus, for example, when angry at oneself, the body may be perceived as unattractive, fat, and often larger.

The body image can be helpful and positive at times. But when problems exist, it can interfere with accurate experiencing of the body. Attempt to be open to the sense data gained from body awareness exercises and to temporarily set aside any preconceptions of what the body is like for the purpose of personal exploration. Concentrate on what is experienced. A new, more accurate and positive body image may become possible.

This chapter has focused attention towards integrated awareness of the body to help correct taken-for-granted misperceptions that interfere with healthy functioning. There are other ways of coordinating and reintegrating mind and body. Self hypnosis using unawareness and anaesthesias of the body may also be used as different paths to the same goal. The creative application of exercises throughout the book will fill in the methodology.

Milton H. Erickson

Ernest L. Rossi

Jerome D. Frank

Josephine R. Hilgard
Ernest R. Hilgard

Emile Coué

Coué and patients in his garden.

Coué conducting a clinic in his house.

Pierre Janet

Jean-Martin Charcot

ANTOINE MESMER,
Docteur en Médecine.

A session of mesmerism in "Le Bacquet"

LE BACQUET DE M. MESMER,
ou Représentation fidelle des Opérations du Magnetisme Animal.

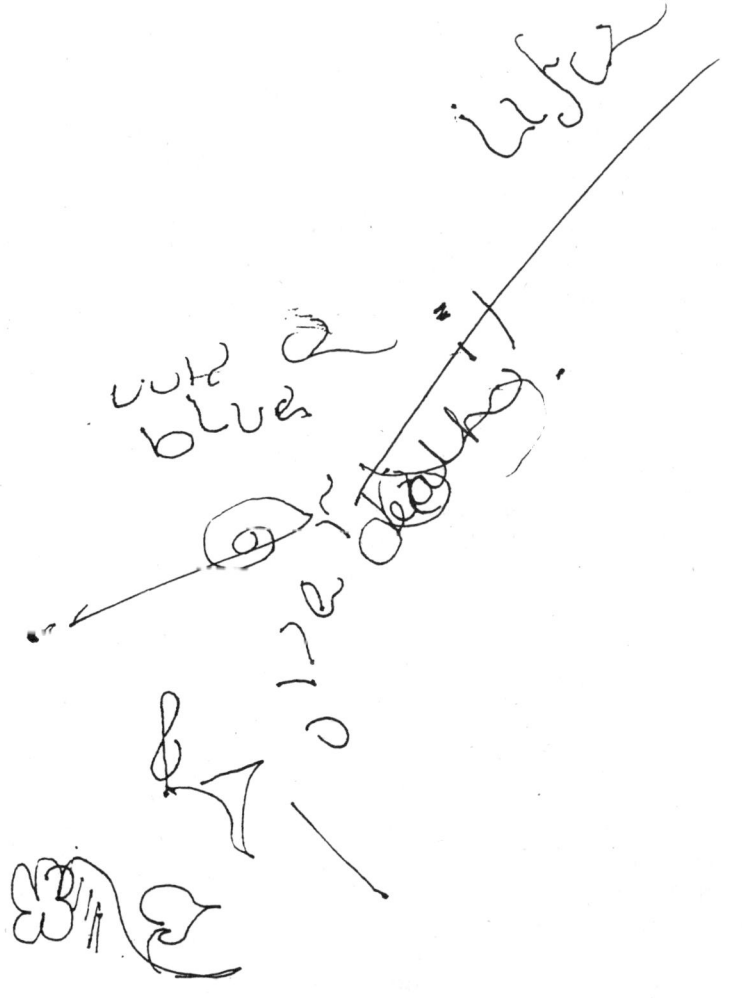

A graduate student grabbling with existential issues.

I know, But I don't ~~liked it~~ either, iguality is ideal, Being what you want to be.

no

yes

A young women in deep hypnotherapy involved in self transformation.

Chapter 5
Steps to Self Hypnosis: Rapport with the Unconscious Mind in Trance

> Fix your thought closely on what is being said, and let your mind enter fully into what is being done, and into what is doing it.
> (Marcus Aurelius)

Now the reader is ready to embark on a journey into self hypnosis, to develop what Jourard called "Learning for oneself."

> Where the learner experiences fascination with some aspect of the world, envisioned in the mode of possibility...Independent learning is the embodiment and implementation of imaginative fascination...he experiences himself as beckoned, challenged, invited, fascinated by the possibility.
> (Jourard, 1968: 112)

The exercises in this chapter can enhance sensitivities to one's own talents for self hypnosis, helping to create possibilities for trance. Preliminary Exercises includes a broad range of exercises to introduce the reader to important building blocks for trance. The reader may find that some exercises seem easier than others. Everyone has their own individual talents: some are good dancers, some can draw accurately, while others are highly creative in other areas. Similarly, we all have unconscious talents. Some people are naturally able to relax, some can easily develop visual hallucinations such as seeing colors when they close their eyes, while others can forget readily. Unconscious abilities are not always recognized as potential talents and may even be considered problems or shortcomings. However, properly applied and worked with, they can become useful hypnotic talents which lead to change and growth in the personality.

Please approach these exercises with an open mind. Consider your efforts to be like a scientific experiment which begins with the gathering of data to be analyzed at a later time. Notice thoughts, experiences, and reactions, but do not pass judgment while collecting the data. Do one exercise at a time, followed by reading of the commentary, or if preferred, read ahead and then return to the exercises. In early attempts one exercise at a sitting is enough. As one gains experience with trance, two or more in one session will seem more appropriate. Do not overload, as there is no advantage in hurrying through. Become sensitive to rhythms and timing.

Read the entire exercise several times, then set the book aside. Make yourself comfortable and try what you remember from the exercise. Do not be concerned with what you forget. Encourage your unconscious to have positive experiences with the exercises.

Preliminary Exercises

Theoretical understanding of the unconscious is only one aspect of the learnings necessary for mastery of self hypnosis. Experiencing is even more primary since the unconscious is sensed experientially.

Preparation for Trance

Before beginning, sit or lie down and relax for a few moments. It is helpful to do this before every exercise, especially if it is your first exercise. People do not usually notice how tense they are during a day. Instead, they adapt and continue on. These exercises attempt to bring you in touch with your level of tension and teach you to let go as you feel able.

As you relax, let your thoughts drift and your attention roam wherever it likes. Try not to get lost in any one thought-path—simply notice associations and follow them. Do this until you notice some settling or calming.

Exercise I:
Everyday Out of Awareness Unconscious

To explore the unconscious as it manifests itself in everyday life, turn your attention to your hands. You probably were not thinking about your hands, but now that we mention them, you become aware of whatever sensations you are having. Perhaps your hands are cold, or feel tingly, or maybe light. You can not accurately guess what you will experience without simply paying attention and waiting for the response. The experience occurs in its own way and in its own time. Sometimes it is interesting to place one hand on each knee and pay attention to the weight of both hands. You might find that one hand is immediately lighter or heavier than the other, or that at first they seem the same, but as you pay attention one becomes heavier than the other. You may be surprised by your unconscious response. While you are waiting for one hand to become lighter you might discover unexpectedly that one hand becomes cooler or maybe you have a new experience of your hand feeling very far away or growing larger. Your unconscious will respond indi-

vidually and the conscious mind does not know how this will be. As you learn to be attentive to your spontaneous responses you will become acquainted with your natural unconscious response which you can learn to develop usefully.

Exercise II: Peripheral Associations

Relax once again. This time you might try to recall how you felt after you completed Exercise I. Try to picture yourself sitting or lying comfortably and remember how your hands felt. As you focus on this experience you will probably find your body beginning to relax a little. Wait until you feel a readiness to try the exercise. While you were thinking about your previous experience you probably had other peripheral thoughts flicker through your mind. Shift your attention to one of the peripheral thoughts or experiences. For example, if it is right before dinner you might notice that you have a vague thought about food. Or perhaps you find yourself thinking about a moment from a pleasant vacation. These less obvious thoughts are continuously present, but you usually do not bring them into consciousness. In this exercise you try to reach for flickers into awareness. These thoughts are like watching a railroad train pass by. You can catch a glimpse of the background between the cars as they pass, but only for an instant and then it is hidden again by the railroad car. Similarly your unconscious thoughts will fleetingly appear in consciousness and then disappear again.

To work with this, let your thoughts drift for a moment. If you notice a flicker into awareness which you cannot quite recognize, invite yourself to have an image or thought which could be a clue. As you become more at ease with your unconscious you will be surprised to discover that your unconscious will supply you with a thought or image which is relevant even if the direct connection is not obvious.

For example, a client came for hypnotherapy to help her deal with a stressful, uncomfortable adaptation to her marriage, job and family. During a trance it was suggested that she have a meaningful image, something which could be helpful in her efforts to understand and outgrow her problems. First she saw lights, mostly white streaks. Then she felt an intense nauseous feeling. After she awoke from the trance, she described this with dismay. She thought that she had not been able to produce an image as had been suggested and worried that she was incapable of imagery. She did not realize that her unconscious had been very responsive. It had expressed itself in a meaningful way in terms of her particular individuality in a mediate rather than an immediate way. The feeling of nausea, just as a dream, held metaphoric significance for her which she would later discover.

Exercise III: Discovering your Perceptual Mode

This exercise is designed to familiarize you with your own spontaneous mode of choice used for perceiving and processing. Bandler and Grinder (1977: 26) pointed out that people function more in one perceptual mode than another. For example, someone might say, "That feels like a good idea, I want to get in touch with that." This person tends to orient kinaesthetically, that is, by feelings and sensations. Another person will say, "I see your point, that looks good." This is a visual orientation. A third type will use metaphors like, "Did you hear about this?" or "I hear that," or "Listen." They usually can recall the sound of someone's voice clearly. They tend to orient auditorily, that is, by hearing. These are the three main perceptual systems of orientation although there are others, such as taste and smell. Also there are differentiations and combinations within each.

Some people do not orient perceptually, but tend to orient conceptually. These kinds of people will say, "I think this is a beautiful day." Experiences are filtered through concepts so that the individual does not notice his perceptions directly. Instead, the concepts of the perceptions are experienced.

People use all of these modes at various times, but typically they process more with one mode than the others. The following exercise can help you determine your mode.

Sit quietly and relax, as in the other exercises. Now recall the moment when you first opened the book. Think about it for a moment, remembering as much about it as you can. Pretend that you can step away from yourself as if you can see yourself remembering. Notice how you recall: 1-do you see a picture of the pages or your hands opening the cover? 2-do you remember how you were feeling, maybe tired, sore, wide awake, happy, or curious about the content. 3-perhaps you remembered the sound of the pages as you turned them or the song that was playing on the radio or street noise. 4-or you may recall what you were thinking—the plans for the day, deliberation over what to eat for your morning meal. If you saw a picture, you probably orient visually. If you felt sensation, you may be more kinaesthetically oriented. If you heard sounds, you tend to orient through the auditory mode. If you experienced a series of thoughts, you may be more conceptual. You may have combinations of these as well. Try this experiment a few times during the day using different memories to double check your results and look for consistent patterns.

Once you determine your mode, use this in the early exercises when there is a choice given. Later, you are encouraged to develop other modes, as each offers a richness in experience and alternative inroads into the unconscious. You may be surprised to discover that you have been delimiting your experiencing this way, and that the other modes of experience can also become comfortable and natural. We use this framework like a map, a way to orient in new territory. Once you become familiar with your unconscious response you will not need to be restricted to this concept.

In the exercises that follow we might suggest that you try to have an image. You might respond with a feeling, thought, or perhaps nothing at all. Keep in mind that these are all legitimate responses which can act as inroads into a working relationship with your unconscious. These links between conscious and unconscious are the keys to successfully learning and applying self hypnosis.

If you have had difficulty thus far with the exercises, shift to Chapter VII on resistances and then return here after you have experimented with defenses and resistance.

The Trance: Self Hypnosis Exercise Series

The reader has done a number or preliminary exercises which have taught some component parts of the hypnotic experience. With this practice plus the theoretical background in mind, the reader is ready to begin learning self hypnosis.

As in many of the previous exercises, the first step is to find a quiet and comfortable place where you can relax without pressure or interruption for at least fifteen minutes. You know that you will be trying your first trance so you might feel excited, nervous, etc. Glance inwardly at your experience now to note any attitudes you might have about doing self hypnosis. Or you might wish to pay attention to your feelings about it, or perhaps listen to yourself and your reactions. Sometimes people have superstitions about the "powers of hypnosis", how it can take over or control the mind. Research indicates that no one has ever been harmed by hypnosis. (Kroger, 1977:104) It is a natural state which allows one to be in touch with inner needs and motivations. Thus people will not do or say anything which contradicts their morals. It is often reassuring to realize that personality tends to remain constant.

Transitions in and out of trance become smoother and easier with practice. At first, after each trance you can help yourself to awaken from trance by counting backwards from 5 to 1. Suggest that with each number you will become more alert and all sensations will return to normal. If you finish and still feel unusual sensations, close your eyes again and go back into trance for a minute or two. Suggest again that your sensations will return to normal and count backwards from 5 to 1 again. As you become more familiar with hypnosis you may not need to count your way out of trance. The experience is most important. We do not tell you to count backwards after each exercise which follows, but you can use this if it helps make the transition to the awake state easier.

Exercise I: Setting Yourself

Imagine for a moment what you expect trance to feel like. People sometimes say that they expect to relax, to feel calm, to have their body become cool or warm, to become light or tingle. If you discovered in the last exercise that you tend to orient visually, try picturing yourself in trance. Would you look relaxed? Are your eyes open or closed? If you felt something, try imagining how you feel.

Notice your response. Does it surprise you or is it consistent with your conscious expectations? If you are surprised, you have probably tapped into an unconscious experience.

Exercise II: Deepening the Trance with Ideomotor Questioning

Review exercises in Chapter II on Suggestion. Experiment with several suggestions; allow your thoughts to drift. Spend some time in this open-ended state. Can you allow yourself to relax even more deeply? You might wonder what it would be like to relax without effort, without tension. Would you feel light all over or a comfortable heaviness? Would the relaxation be warm or cool? Experiment with an open, questioning attitude and be curious about your response.

The trance experience is not always easy to recognize at first. You may have noticed that you were relaxed and calm but may feel that this is not anything unusual or different from an ordinary waking state. Confirmation that trance is happening helps to intensify the experience and leads to an increase in trance abilities. Erickson and Rossi refer to this as "trance ratification", of which ideomotor signalling is one example.

Close your eyes and relax once again. Sit or lie so that your hands rest either on your legs or by your side. Experiment with one of the previous exercises to which you felt responsive. Invite yourself to become even more relaxed than before. Once you feel comfortable focus your attention on your hands. Consider how frequently people move their hands in conversation without thinking about it. Sometimes the gesture is even more meaningful than the words. Do you talk with your hands?

Now, ask your unconscious a yes or no question. Designate one hand as a "yes" and the other hand as a "no." Choose a question for which you do not have the answer, such as: Would my unconscious like my legs to relax? Could I feel tingling in my fingertips? Can I have an interesting pleasant memory? Could I see colors when I close my eyes? Now, wait and pay close attention to your hands. Do not try to move them, simply notice. Sometimes people feel tingling, sometimes one hand will feel lighter or the other heavier. Sometimes a person will notice warmth or coolness. Still others will feel a finger raise in one hand or the other or maybe a feeling jumps from one hand to the other and back again. After a little while you will know what your response has been and in which hand. If you felt something in your hand, your unconscious answered the question.

This exercise may not be what you expected or it may come out exactly as you predicted. These mysteries make communicating with your unconscious mind interesting. Your conscious mind does not know what your unconscious mind already knows. Milton Erickson often said, "Your unconscious mind knows more than you do."

Exercise III: Body Image Alterations

People take the body image for granted as a fixed reality. Except perhaps when one has the flu, changes in the body experience often are not noticed. Chapter IV dealt with this in relation to the unconscious. Hypnosis can allow you to experience and work with body image, to creatively apply these learnings to related problems.

Sit or lie down quietly, relaxing. Let all of your muscles settle. In this exercise it is helpful to experience a very deep and comfortable relaxation of tension. Think back on the preliminary exercises and recall whether you had a stronger auditory (hearing), visual (seeing), kinesthetic (feeling), or conceptual (thinking) response. You can use your preferred mode to achieve the maximal relaxation for you at this point. Your unconscious will regulate the level, so do not be consciously concerned about this; rather, try not to inhibit the natural unconscious response from occurring. This can be done partly by an honest curiosity about what this experience will be like, wondering how you will feel, and waiting for the response.

Auditory

Recall a sound of nature, like the ocean waves, a bubbling brook, the quiet of a winter's snow fall, the wind rustling through the trees, or any other sound which you have enjoyed. Focus your attention on this but do not push the image. Simply wait for it to fill out, to become even fuller or perhaps to alter in some way which you do not expect. While you listen, your body can relax even deeper. Your muscles settle and you can let go of any unnecessary tension. Continue listening and allow any other images, thoughts, or feelings to develop as well. Deepen the experience as you feel ready and continue to relax deeply.

Visual

Recall an image or a place you have been and really enjoyed. Perhaps a vacation spot, a hideaway in the mountains, a secluded beach, a forest. Picture the beauty; look at the colors; walk around and reacquaint yourself with it. You would be relaxed if you went there and so your body can relax now as you picture this experience. You might see these images vividly or they could be vague wisps of pictures and colors flickering past. However they appear, you can ask your unconscious to enhance the experience with a very comfortable feeling of relaxation all over. You can picture yourself relaxing even more and wonder how deeply relaxed you can become.

Kinaesthetic

You will probably find your attention wandering to the feelings in your body. As you begin to relax, focus your attention on a very nice feeling of calm, both inner and outer; ask all of your muscles to settle. You can recall an experience when you felt totally at ease, calm, and comfortable. Recall where you were, as in the previous mode exercises, but focus on the experience you had in your body, the memory of the calmness or happiness you felt there. You may find yourself naturally filling out the details with memories of the place, events which transpired, or other relevant details. Whatever your unconscious comes up with, you can follow it with *curiosity and interest in just what it would be like to relax even deeper than you ever have before. Wait for the response as you continue to imagine that calm, comfortable feeling.*

Conceptual

Sit quietly and begin relaxing. Let your thoughts drift without interfering with them. As your thoughts flow however they will, watch them but do not interfere. This is similar to watching a play. You follow it carefully but do not step on stage to alter the action. You are attentive and interested without interfering. Similarly, here you carefully attend to your own flow of associations without judging the content or directing in any way. As you do this, your body can relax very comfortably without your even quite noticing it.

Now that you have relaxed, you are ready to try an interesting set of exercises in body alterations. People take their experience of their body for granted and assume it to be accurate. (See Chapter IV) However, these sensations are malleable. Such alterations can foster new developments and learnings for the personality in general.

Hand Levitation

The experience of a lightness and movement developing in a finger, hand, or arm is a classic hypnotic phenomenon called hand levitation. The finger, hand, or arm feels as if it is moving by itself; you do not need to do anything in particular except to allow it to occur naturally. People who are kinaesthetic may find this easier to do, but anyone can experience it with time. It is done by gathering momentum, building each experience upon the next. All that you have already learned helps to shape your response. These exercises can be repeated as often as you like, at different sessions.

Exercise in Hand Levitation

For this exercise it is helpful to sit or lie in such a way that your hands and arms are comfortably unencumbered. If you are sitting, let a hand rest on each knee. If you are lying down, place your hands either by your side or across your body, but do not place one hand over the other. Let your body relax and focus your attention on your hands. Notice any experience you might begin to have. One common feeling is a tingling in the fingertips. You might compare your two hands as to whether one feels lighter, heavier, warmer, or cooler. Stay with the experience and ask your unconscious what it would be like for the tingling, warming, or whatever you feel, to begin to lead to a feeling of lightness. It might feel like something is tugging on a finger, thumb, or hand, as if a helium balloon is tied to the finger or wrist, or it might be a very nice lightness which gets lighter and lighter with every breath. Perhaps the tingling could increase and bring about a feeling for movement which you do not inhibit. Follow this experience, however it manifests for you and let your fingers begin to raise. Stay with it and invite the lightness to increase and the hand to raise even higher. You might like to suggest that your hand goes all the way up to touch your face. When it does you can feel more deeply relaxed than you have before in trance.

Give yourself time to allow these sensations to develop. Look, listen, and sense your particular response. You do not know which hand will respond and just what it will be like, but you can, as in previous exercises, become increasingly curious as to how your unconscious will respond. Many creative variations are possible.

A client underwent hypnosis to learn to control his temper. He was a lawyer and felt that his anger interfered with his professional and personal life. Before the trance, hand levitation was discussed as one hypnotic phenomenon. He said he was curious to try it even though he thought it would be very difficult to learn. He experienced a comfortable trance and even smiled as his muscles relaxed. Hand levitation was suggested similarly to how it is described above. His hands barely moved if at all, but his face was slightly flushed and a few bead of sweat appeared on his brow. Upon awakening he recounted what he referred to as a "marvelous experience." He said that the levitation was so intense that he was doing jumping jacks! The experience was vivid and he felt as if he had exerted tremendous energy. He was extremely pleased to realize that he could have an intense experience without acting it out. This was pivotal in the moderation of his temper.

An hypnotic phenomenon does not always correlate with what it seems to be. It can be a metaphor, a symbol, or even an inspiration for growth and learnings.

Visual Imagery and Hallucination

Visual experiences in trance are a natural phenomenon of hypnosis. Everyone can learn to have visual experiences even though it might be easier for some than for others.

A classic method for entering trance is by using the visual faculty. The hypnotic subject is encouraged to look at an hypnotic object, such as a crystal ball or a lit candle. However, any object which interests you will do. The authors often have used abstract paintings. Erickson had a quartz crystal to direct the gaze to. Be imaginative.

Exercise in Hallucination

To begin, look at the object carefully. Study it, noticing all its components, the colors, the shapes. Next look at the outline, then the interior. Watch very carefully, focusing all your attention on the object. As you concentrate fully on it, your thoughts can drift. Think about the object, look at the object, study it. As you watch, you can let your body relax, your breathing rate settle. After you have studied all the different components let your eyes move around the object. Notice if you can see any alterations in the object as you watch. You may see a blurring, a change in the colors or an alteration in shape. Perhaps you are noticing aspects which you did not see before, or maybe the object does appear to alter. Try suggesting an alteration which you would be curious to experience and wait for your response. Meanwhile, you can enjoy a lessening of tension and a comfortable feeling all over.

Looking at an external object is often done as an hypnotic technique. However, hypnosis, being an inner experience, can be far more powerfully achieved for some by an image from within.

Exercise in Inner Imagery

In this exercise, you can begin by relaxing your body as before. You might like to try this exercise following the previous one. As you are looking at your chosen object, you can suggest that your eyelids could become heavy. Think about your eyelids becoming heavier and heavier, wait for the sensation of your eyes wanting to close, and then allow your eyelids to close. An alternative method is to simply close your eyes, relaxing your eyelids, allowing your entire body to relax very deeply.

The reader has experimented earlier with inner imagery, picturing a place, a scene, a memory. But it is also possible to visualize color in formless, abstract, or symbolic form. At first the color may appear as just one shade. Gradually it could alter in its shade, depth, or even change colors. Sometimes people see a kaleidoscope of color; other times it is simply white or black, afterimages, lights, or streaks. Experiment with offering a suggestion for a color you would like to experience. Wait for your response. Watch it evolve.

Anaesthesia & Hyperaesthesia

Anaesthesia is a well documented hypnotic phenomenon. It has been used for surgery as the sole anesthetic. For example, there is an educational film from the 1950's showing a woman undergoing her fourth Cesarean birth under hypnosis with no pain. Hypnosis was used predominantly in surgery before the discovery of chloroform, as pointed out in Chapter 1.

Classically anaesthesia has been produced by direct suggestion. However, this relies upon the subject being suggestible. As has been discussed, hypnotic effectiveness does not depend upon suggestibility. Anaesthesia can be produced by other means.

Motivation can enhance the ability to produce anaesthesia. A client who was working on an intense personality change used hypnosis occasionally to relax. She did not think she was very good at it and even doubted its efficacy. She was an intelligent girl in her late twenties. She suffered from intense anxiety. She felt stuck in an uncomfortable job and living situation. She tended to be judgmental, especially toward herself. During the course of treatment she had to get a tooth extracted. She decided to give the hypnosis a try without the use of novocaine. She had no idea how she would implement the anaesthesia. She reported at her session following the dental work that she felt nervous about the operation, but that she spontaneously imagined little creatures in her mouth rolling big balls of pain away. As she viewed this image she found the pain leaving. She handled the whole thing during and after surprisingly well. She had not expected to use an image, especially such a seemingly silly one.

Exercise in Anaesthesia with Direct Suggestion

Find a comfortable trance, suggesting relaxation and comfort of the body. Decide where you would like to produce the anaesthesia: a hand? head? foot? etc. Next you can give yourself a suggestion in a mode which you have used successfully before, or you might want to experiment with something new. You could recall a time when you were out in very cold temperatures, and after a period of time your nose and cheeks became so cold that they were numb. Recall the tingling followed by a nothing feeling which you might have felt. Suggest that the body part is tingling as it becomes colder and colder until you can no longer feel it.

Sometimes you can produce anaesthesia by dissociating from that body part. Imagine that your hand, arm, or wherever you have chosen, is feeling far away from the rest of your body. You might feel as if the hand is growing in size at first and then seems to take on an unreal or distant quality. Some subjects have watched themselves from a distance. One client felt like he left his body at the session and went to the beach. Some people feel tingly or temperature alterations before the hand or arm begins to feel distant or numb.

Exercise in Dissociation for Anaesthesia

Picture yourself going into trance. Watch your eyes close and thoughts drift. Notice whether your body can move or not, just how comfortable you can be. Once you feel fully relaxed, notice that you are watching yourself and are dissociated from direct body experience via your perceptual mode.

Experiment with these different approaches and then wait for your response. You will probably be curious to discover how your unconscious will want to react. You can test yourself once you feel that you have achieved an adequate anaesthesia by touching the anaesthetized body part. If you feel unable to move, compare the sensation in the anaesthetized arm, leg, etc. to that of an unanaesthesized part.

Hyperaesthesia

Many people know about hypnosis and anaesthesia, but few people realize that hypnosis can also enhance sensations. This can be very useful in some circumstances. A young man of 27 years, teeming with excess energy, came for hypnotherapy. He had lost his job and decided to start his own business working with machinery. He spoke quickly, moved around during the sessions, and complained of being "hyper". In his new business, he complained that sometimes he would miss a small detail which caused him to have to return to the job site to redo the work. All profit was lost and at times it even cost him money to complete the job.

He learned to go into trance and found himself enjoying the calm and relaxation of hypnosis. In trance it was suggested that he imagine a place where he felt very comfortable. He thought of the woods near where he grew up. He recalled every detail: the woods noises, the smell of the leaves and plants, the colors of the sun shining through the trees. He searched back in his memory to carefully recall many details, focusing all his energy on sensitizing himself to the experience. The week after this exercise he reported that he had been surprised to discover something new. Seemingly automatically, he found himself listening intently, looking carefully, and noticing details in the machinery he was fixing. He reported that he could hear minute sounds which indicated where the malfunction occurred. His exacting attentiveness had resulted in a week with no callbacks, no errors. The learnings he had begun in trance were enhanced by asking him to feel his shin, notice how long his arms were, his legs, to feel his breathing. He learned to become so sensitive in trance that he could feel a slight breeze or a minute touch to his arm. The ability to produce hyperaesthesia can be developed on your own in trance.

Exercise:

Begin with a memory, perhaps a place or an experience which you enjoyed or one which happened very re-

cently. Now consider what it would be like to recall details of the experience which you had forgotten. Concentrate on sense memories such as taste, smell, touch, or sound. Was there a bird or cricket chirping? Did the waves pound at the ocean? Or perhaps you can recall the sound of someone's voice? Wait for a memory to appear. Request that it become even clearer. We will develop these preliminary skills further in Chapter 8 for specific applications.

Time Distortion

Another natural ability of the unconscious is time distortion. Everyone has had the experience of the minutes slowly ticking, waiting in line, sitting through a dull class, or enduring a boring dinner party. Conversely, there are times when the hours pass too quickly. These are both examples of the mind's natural ability to alter the experience of time.

If the average person were asked to define time, he would probably think of time as it seems on a clock. However, suppose a class of students were asked how long the duration of a class session seemed. The answers would vary greatly. The interested, involved student would probably report a different seeming duration than the bored disinterested student. The reader might insist that fifty minutes is a fixed time interval. But time distortion occurs when the seeming duration of a time interval is different from the clock time of that interval. Time distortion can appear to be either shorter or longer, depending upon the experience. Both are useful, natural, and can be utilized for creative and therapeutic applications.

Milton Erickson and Linn F. Cooper (Cooper & Erickson, 1982: 20-22) did extensive research on this phenomenon. They carefully set up experimental definitions of time distortion to refer to the discrepancy between clock time and experiential time on a given time interval. One experiment instructed a trance subject to go to a cotton field and pick four rows of cotton, counting the bolls as she picked them, one at a time. The subject was not to hurry and was to raise her hand when she finished. The subject raised her hand 217 seconds after starting and reported 719 cotton bolls. She stated that she seemed to have been working for one hour and twenty minutes. When asked to demonstrate by counting aloud, the rate she counted was 56 bolls in one minute.

The second experiment involved the same task except that the experimenter put a time limit on the task. The time allotted was three seconds. The subject reported that she had picked 862 bolls and that it seemed like an entire hour and twenty minutes.

The following exercises will illustrate both the experience of time going faster, and that of time slowing down. Both have their applications and uses. For example, speeding up the experience of time can be very useful in pain control, whereas slowing it down can make it possible to learn to accomplish more efficiently.

Preliminary Exercise

Go into trance, relax, and be comfortable. Think about time for a moment. Picture the hands of a clock and watch them move for a five minute period. Wonder whether you could tell the difference between 32 minutes and 33 minutes, or if you could distinguish an interval of 5 seconds from 6. Think about a time when you were very bored and time seemed to move very slowly. Waiting for something to occur can give such an experience. Think of others. Now recall a time when the hours passed so quickly that looking back it seemed over before it started. Holidays often leave people with this experience. Let your mind drift, associations flow, and relax very deeply. When you are ready, let your mind clear for a moment. Perhaps you would like to imagine a lake settling, where all the mud sinks to the bottom. The water becomes crystal clear, like your mind can be. When you are ready, wake up refreshed and alert.

Exercise: Slowing down Time

For this exercise, you can give yourself an experience in time distortion. Find a quiet place outdoors where you can walk comfortably and alone (or without speaking if you are with someone) for what feels like 15 minutes. Allow your mind to drift freely. Do not try to direct your attention anywhere in particular. When you believe 15 minutes have passed, stop and check your watch. Immediately following, go take a walk in a place which is busy and congested also for what feels like 15 minutes. Again, let your thoughts drift and do not look at your watch until you think you have walked for 15 minutes. Afterwards, notice what you experienced and return home. If you have noted a difference between experienced time and clock time you have had an experience of time distortion. Were there differences between the two walks in terms of time? Feelings? Comfort level?

Exercise II

Next available session time find a comfortable place to sit and relax. Allow yourself to go comfortably into trance. Once you feel that you have found an inner calmness, suggest that you recall your two walks. Think back on the surroundings of each one, one at a time, and try to visualize yourself there again. Some people will actually feel as if they are re-enacting the walk. Assure yourself that you have all the time you need to take the walks, and do not rush. Follow this procedure for each of the two walks. When you have completed both, wake up, noting how long each walk seemed to take. Check the time on the clock.

Exercise III

Check the clock before you go into trance. Let an image occur to you, any image or scene. As you watch, other images will occur, one after another. Let these images become as vivid as they can until you feel as if you are right there in the scene. Follow the scene until you feel ready to clear your mind of all images. You might suggest a blank, a black nothingness, or bright light. Play with the possibilities as you wait for your response and enjoy a deep relaxation. When you are ready, awaken relaxed and refreshed. Note how long you felt this took, then check the time. Repeat this exercise a few times at different sessions, attempting to make the images more and more vivid.

Exercise IV

In this exercise you will go into trance and visualize yourself doing an activity which normally takes a fixed amount of clock time to complete. Relax and allow your body to settle into trance. You can choose from one of the following three activities, or choose one of your own: 1) Swim laps or jog, ride a bike, etc. for 15-20 minutes. 2) Cook breakfast including all preparations for 15-20 minutes. (Let someone else do the dishes) 3) Watch the first quarter of a football game (or soccer match or one inning of baseball, or any other favorite sport.) Another possibility is to watch the first act of a play you enjoy.

You have practiced this kind of thing several times. Make your choice of which task you will be doing. If you have another activity which takes about 15-20 minutes, this will be fine. The point is to choose something and allow yourself to become intensely interested in performing it. Tell yourself to take your time and work to the best of your ability. Do not hurry.

> *Try to be thorough. When you have found a comfortable level of trance, begin the activity. Remember to note the time before you go into trance and when you awaken. When you have finished, clear your mind and then wake up refreshed and alert. You can repeat this exercise a few times at various sittings. Try to use what feels like 15 or 20 minutes at each sitting. If you find that there is a discrepancy between the clock time and the experienced time, you have had an experience of time distortion.*

Frequently people will experience time expansion with these exercises. However, both time expansion and time constriction are useful tools. One of our clients had an experience with time distortion which clarifies its surprising benefits. She wanted to lose weight. She was working for a utilities company while she was going to school in the evenings to become a nurse. She told us that she disliked her job and felt like the time dragged by each day. She felt that she barely had any time for herself or her school work. Some co-workers who were also consulting the authors for hypnosis at the time reported that she was very grumpy and hard to get along with at work.

She went into a very deep trance during treatment and had total amnesia for the trance experience. During her sessions she was taught time distortion similar to the exercises in this chapter. Her unconscious spontaneously came up with a very creative solution to her dilemmas. At her next session she reported that she had a surprising experience. She found that each day at work that week the days had just sped by. But strangely when she got home in the evening she felt as if she had all the time in the world. As the weeks passed she found that much to her surprise work grew to be more and more pleasant for her. She was happier and more relaxed since she knew she would have plenty of time after work to do what she wanted for her career and household. Her fellow workers experienced her as being much friendlier and easier to get along with. By the time she had finished school and was ready to quit her job she felt sorry to leave and her co-workers said they would miss her. This illustration shows how the unconscious can apply hypnotic skills when given the invitation to do so.

Chapter Summary

In this chapter you have experimented with many different hypnotic possibilities. Hopefully, you have approached the exercises with an openness to your individual abilities, developing and enlarging upon these skills. You may begin to see how areas of difficulties and resistance can often be developed into assets. How to work with resistance will be described in Chapter 7. You can return to these basic exercises over and over. This adds to and embellishes upon the learnings you have begun until eventually trance becomes a comfortable and readily available tool.

Chapter 6 helps to apply some of these trance learnings to everyday life. Links can be made both theoretically and practically. In Chapter 8 the reader can make specific applications to many areas using carefully set out techniques of self hypnosis. Hopefully the trance abilities developed in the earlier chapters will help in accomplishing specific goals.

Chapter 6
The Unlearning of Learning, and the Learning of Unlearning

> You can know something, but not understand it, and then again, you can understand something, but you don't know what it is.
>
> (Milton Erickson)

Learning Theories

Learning takes place all through life. Things can be learned in one context and then applied in another, creatively. Perls (1969) often said, "Learning is the discovery that something is possible". In this kind of learning, there is insight and discovery of new meanings and potentials.

There have been many volumes written on learning theory. For the purpose of this book and its length, only a brief selection from learning theories will be given. The reader will be encouraged to experiment with exercises applying learning theory principles. When combined with some of the techniques presented in Chapter 7, it is hoped that the reader can make his self hypnotic learnings a useful and pragmatic addition to his everyday life.

Learning, from the Concrete to the Abstract

Montessori learning theory (1964) views the natural flow of growth as moving from the concrete to the abstract. The child, for example, playing with three objects comes to realize the concepts of objects and their number. In learning addition, groups of objects are manipulated prior to learning addition tables. There is natural learning by doing. Concepts are abstracted from actual demonstrations. Goldstein developed a concrete to abstract theory which he applied in testing brain damage. He found that brain-damaged patients cannot abstract: they can point to things, but not say what they are. This resembles the developmental process in indirect hypnotherapy. The learner evolves from the simplest unconscious abilities to more complex abstract applications. Understanding and mastery of trance phenomena comes through first hand experiencing and self experimentation. Explore the experience. Then, conceptualize about it, if you want to.

Incidental Learning

Incidental learning is an example of the unconscious effortlessly at work. Often when someone is helping another to learn material for school, he might question him from the book repetitively. Afterwards, the helper finds, much to his surprise, that he has learned the material as well as or better than the student. People learn incidentally in many realms without conscious effort.

Generalization of Learning

Generalization of learning and transfer from the original context to another concrete context is important if learning is to have relevance. Hilgard noted (1968) that transference in psychoanalysis is closely akin to transfer and generalization in learning theory. When basic learning has taken place, it is necessary to generalize or transfer that learning to other contexts to make use of that learning and make it one's own.

Guthrie, (1935) postulated that learning is mainly linking or associating ideas. Two events that take place together in time, especially if it happens regularly, tend to be linked or associated. When going back to old situations, memory often clearly indicates this: people are reminded of the old situations and events when they re-experience the place or hear an old song on the radio.

Creative learning can take the patterns from one context of meaning and apply them in another. Many creative and inventive people draw meaningful patterns from widely divergent areas of interest. Freud, as a famous example, was a great student of archeology. He considered it his second love, only surpassed by psychoanalysis. Many do not recognize how extensively his psychoanalytical theories drew from archeology. Indeed, he drew from his understandings of archeology, reconstructing the causes and precursors of the present problem from the psychological relics of the past.

At first, when positive learning takes place, the learning is context bound. If a series of similar learning contexts are experienced, the rate of learning accelerates. This is deuterolearning (Bateson). People speak of this phenomenon in learning another language. The second language takes a long time, the third less, the fourth is even quicker, and the twentieth is very rapid. Nonsense syllables by the third or fourth trial can be learned more rapidly than the first trial.

Pavlovian Conditioning

In Pavlovian or classical conditioning there is a regular pairing or association of the learned stimulus with another stimulus that automatically and naturally brings about a certain response. The classic example of Pavlovian conditioning is ringing a bell immediately before presenting a dog with food. The dog salivates in a reflex response to the food, and soon he associates bell ringing with food. Then, merely ringing a bell makes the dog salivate. The dog has no sense that he can have any influence on the outcome of feeding or not: he merely learns that ringing a bell leads to food, and thus responds to that expectancy or signal. This eventually diminishes in time if the food does not follow bell ringing for a period of time. Perhaps a new connection is learned.

Those who subscribe to this theory assume that alcoholism, overeating, smoking, phobias, and other problems can be understood as faulty learnings. The person afraid of snakes, for example, has learned to associate snakes with anxiety. Whenever they see a snake, they feel anxiety and fear. The compulsive overeater associates food with compulsive eating behavior or stress with going to the refrigerator. Successful treatment methods in this approach require that the patient regularly experience the problematic stimulus e.g. alcohol, chocolate, snakes, etc. without permitting the usual behavior to follow, or else pairing with a different response altogether.

Analytical Learning

In conjunction with this, some therapists believe that one should work on the deeper motivations and conflicts as well. In other words, it helps to want to change and to feel hopeful and positive about the techniques. Experts differ widely in their opinions whether working through conflicts in the assumptive world is necessary. Most theorists who subscribe to the analytical approaches believe that change is impossible without working through the deeper level conflict and concerns. Their rationale involves a "tension reduction" model of what a problem is: conflicts cause tension; conflict and tension are expressed symbolically in symptoms such as overeating, phobias, and other problems. Thus it is important to deal with the underlying conflict that fuels the symptom with energy and meaning. Research on the outcome of psychotherapy does not consistently support any one method or approach in all circumstances for all individuals. A balanced treatment regime that takes the individuality into account is probably best. Research in outcome studies does indicate that self-selection of the treatment method leads to better results in achieving therapeutic goals. (Frank, et.al., 1978:172-3) Thus, this book presents several methods for working with difficulties and asks that the reader use what is best for him.

Learning theorists think of troublesome conflicts as faulty learnings that can be unlearned, forgotten, or exchanged for new learnings. Instrumental conditioning or learning theories take a different approach from the analytical view in terms of how learning takes place.

Reinforcement and Frame of Reference

When learning a behavior, "reinforcement" or a "reward" is presented after successful performance. Behavior which approaches the appropriate, requested behaviors is rewarded consistently until a connection or association is made between the learning pattern and the reinforcement. The subject learns that his efforts can bring rewards or their absence. Thorndike was the forerunner of this, with his concept of satisfiers or positive rewards which he believed tend to strengthen a response, and annoyers or negative rewards which tend to weaken or discourage it. (Thorndike, 1977) These learnings tend to remain in context. However, as Bateson has stated, there are also "context markers" or ways by which the situation is defined and pointed out as what it is. When a mouse is put in a maze, it is clear to the mouse after being exposed to this kind of situation regularly that it is expected by the experimenter not to just sit there, nor to just clean itself. The situation is a learning or performance situation, and the mouse is ready or expectantly oriented soon after being placed there.

The context marker, or the way in which a situation is pointed out, becomes what we have earlier referred to as the "frame of reference" or orientation. These terms are used frequently by Erickson and Rossi in their Indirect Hypnotherapy model. After regular repeated experiences, a frame of reference becomes quite taken for granted. When put in other similar kinds of puzzle boxes, the mouse gets quicker to respond by appropriate behavior.

In essence, as you learn how to learn, you learn a point of view or frame of reference, a definition of the situation, by how it has been pointed out. In creative learning, you learn to transcend the context or frame of reference and discover other contexts or points of view by which to understand the learning. Thus, a cabinetmaker learns to think about and construct cabinets in learning his trade, and he also learns a point of view during the process that becomes taken for granted, a context marker. He would find it difficult to become a rough framing carpenter, since even though both work with wood and measurements, there is another point of view in that trade: get it done fast, work rapidly with certain tolerances for gaps and accuracy. These tolerances would never be acceptable for cabinetmaking where exactness and smooth finishes are expected.

There is value in expanding your point of view in an area so that you can achieve different results. To continue the example, the cabinetmaker who has learned framing originally, can include this in his cabinet designs in various ways. He can grow in design by incorporating the point of view of different artists and artisans in adding subtlety to textures, shapes, finish, and so on. Change involves the ability to shift the point of view so that new possibilities can emerge.

A musician who paints will likely have a flow of harmony and composition that is unique. There is an abstract painter who has been influenced by classical music. She considers herself a concert violinist first, a painter second.

The point of view taken affects what is learned as well as the options for how to use what is learned. The mathematics teacher who is arrogant and condescending may unintentionally and indirectly give a certain frame of reference to his students. Some may be repelled and threatened by his attitudes toward math and their errors, and become insecure about the subject. Others may identify with it, admiringly. Still others may manage to separate the subject somehow from the teacher, and find a rationale to explain or deal with it. Years later, when relearning math as an adult, or using it, the context in which it was learned is frequently recalled. However, with other experiences in math or related subjects, the learning context may be transcended.

The conscious and unconscious, as in the gestalt formulations, may be thought of as figure/background phenomena.

When the context is transcended, a new, more comprehensive context is created that includes more possibilities.

Desensitization

There is another side to the learning process that is basic in working it into your everyday life: the processes known as desensitization and re-education. Desensitization and reeducation are terms that have varied meanings due to their connotations. Wolpe worked out a method widely used in behavior therapy known as "systematic desensitization" as part of reciprocal inhibition to erase a habit pattern that is problematic. A response that is incompatible with the unwanted response is cultivated, to neutralize the unwanted response by reciprocal action.

Systematic desensitization involves the cultivation of deep relaxation during a usually disturbing situation, by practice and therapist feedback on the depth of relaxation. A hierarchy or gradient of stimuli approaching the problematic learning or habit pattern of response is set up to ease the client gradually into handling the difficulty. As an example, a phobia of snakes might be confronted gradually, from the least threatening, being a mile away from a garter snake, to most threatening, holding a snake. The patient is first relaxed, then presented with the least threatening stimulus, often purely imaginatively. When some anxiety or fear arises, the person relaxes until the fear or anxiety is no longer experienced as uncomfortable. Then the patient is encouraged to approach the most feared and threatened situation one step at a time while he cultivates a calm, relaxed state. Of course, hypnosis can be used and in principle it is difficult to say that suggestion and hypnosis are not primary in the process, since visualization, suggestion, and relaxation are involved. Erickson found in early experiments on the nature of hypnosis, (Erickson, 1964) that carefully visualizing and imagining a simple action, such as picking up pieces of fruit, examining them carefully, and putting them down, resulted for the majority of subjects in deep trances with hallucinations. (Erickson, 1980)

Suggestion and expectation play a major part in Behavior Therapies. Therapists build expectation for cure, and suggest results. The Hopkins Researchers found favorable expectations helpful in producing change and relief of symptoms. (Frank et. al., 1978)

Guthrie describes methods for preventing a response to a stimulus. (1938) One approach is to present the stimulus at such a low intensity that it does not evoke the response. Then, gradually, the stimulus intensity is increased or allowed to amplify while carefully ensuring that the threshold of response is not reached, so that tolerance develops.

Another method is to present the stimulus cues while at the same time preventing the response from taking place either directly by inhibition or else by distraction with some other stimulus as well. For example, clients were unaware of loud, continuous construction noise next door during their quiet calming hypnosis sessions, even though most of the conversation was seemingly drowned out., They were surprised when the noise was mentioned after. Relaxing and concentrating on inner concerns led to unawareness of disturbing stimuli and no discomfort later. They often reported more tolerance to discomfort in general following treatment. There may have been a deconditioning or desensitization process that took place. Then, spontaneously occurring reeducation became possible as they discovered the ability to comfortably tolerate discomfort and distraction. New habits of response may soon be established, based in these discoveries of possibilities.

There are many other creative uses of learning theory and methods that can be applied in hypnotherapy. Experimentation is the best way to find applications.

Fascination and deep absorption in learning for oneself can result from being interested and imaginatively involved. Immersion in learning permits rapid, effortless memorization and deep retention of material, as well as easy accessibility. Most people have had a time when they became enthralled with learning something, due to an inspiring, wonderful teacher or some personal identification with the ideas or material. Getting a high grade or being applauded for excellence in performance became secondary to the involvement.

Paradoxically an "A" grade often follows easily. It can be intrinsically rewarding just to learn or do something interesting, and very non-rewarding or punishing to learn to do something uninteresting. In these cases it is helpful to search for the value in it, to discover interests which might be related.

Exercise using Learning Theory

In the following exercises pick a minor behavior which you would like to change. These exercises are intended to offer a taste of working with yourself behaviorally which will be used in combination with self hypnosis in Chapter 8.

Learning how to learn is an essential component of most self help. Begin by choosing an area which you would like to improve in yourself. For example, we will describe working on being more organized on one's household. Your usual approach to this might be to vow that you will be more organized and have a period of time in which you show improvement before you slip back to your old ways. During the time that you are involved with this exercise, do not make any special efforts to organize your house. instead, go to a book store or library and look at books written on being organized. Think about the different ideas offered. Next, visit a friend who is, in your opinion, organized. Talk to him about it; ask him how he is able to accomplish this. All the while, think about organization. Find out how a business is organized. If you do not know anyone who has their own business, ask a local store owner where you shop. After about a week's exploration of the topic you can pick one area of your house to organize. Make it a small section, perhaps a drawer which holds the bills, or a sewing box, or some other limited area. As you do this, think about what you have learned. If this is successful over time, add something else to organize. If not, go back to your research. As you become more at home in learning about the topic you will find that it becomes easier to make the necessary changes.

Independent learning goes further, in that the learner frees himself from the momentum and inertia of previous ways of behaving and experiencing. People tend to follow the pathways that earlier learnings have carved out, taking it for granted that "That's the way it is". It is as if your car begins to make a funny noise. You don't notice it at first, then, eventually you become aware of a sound you had not heard before. You think, "Oh well, this car is getting older", and continue driving. The radiator overheats and you add water at the nearest gas station. You realize that the noise is coming from the radiator and consider buying stop-leak. You keep refilling the radiator whenever it runs out of water and carry a water jug with you everywhere. You are late to three appointments on different occasions because the car overheats and you have to stop to fill it. Finally after months of this you bring the car in to be fixed. The mechanic informs you that you have a cracked block as well as needing a new radiator. You leave with a $650.00 bill and confirmation of your belief. You were so convinced that your car was an old problem, you did not bother to deal with the radiator at its earliest stage when the repair could have been easy and inexpensive. People often do this in other areas, basing inadequate coping on the belief that there are no other options. Anticipation would have prevented this.

While growing up people become accustomed to a certain way of being. This becomes accepted and interpreted as the way life works. Husserl, phenomenological philosopher of the early 1900's, called this the natural world of experiencing, the "Life World." As was discussed in Chapter 3, the life worldview can also limit the individual to a set of assumptions, beliefs, attitudes, and values that have been acquired. This can be a valuable context from one point of view, to orient, cope, and achieve meaningful goals. It can also serve as a constricting or negative limitation when the assumptions are inhibiting and narrow, "I can't do this", "I'm not this or that sort of person".

Hypnosis can be used to sidestep and elude such definitions, so that discovery of how to accomplish something becomes possible. Conscious and unconscious understandings have a variety of ways of being integrated. Erickson pointed out that it is possible to have a conscious and unconscious understanding which may differ. Rossi, (1981) in a more recent book, highlighted the importance of integrating conscious and unconscious understandings as expressed in Erickson's earlier work. Later, in such volumes as *Hypnotic Realities* (1976) and *Hypnotherapy Casebook* (1979) Erickson considered the essence of therapy to be the changes brought about in the patient. Integration of conscious with unconscious understandings was not axiomatic: indeed, he believed that often the conscious mind interferes and imposes limitations on the unconscious potential of the patient.

Analytic theory classically held that insight was essential for permanent change to take place. Modern dynamic hypnotherapy draws from the best of these concepts. However, there are other alternatives to integrating unconscious learnings into everyday life. People vary on how to best apply hypnotic learnings. For some it is best left to the unconscious, for others, behavioral techniques are very effective, while still others find analysis helps. In this chapter the reader is encouraged to experiment in order to discover which ways prove individually useful.

The Conscious-Unconscious Balance

People differ in the balance of conscious with unconscious understandings. Wolberg points out that "ego strength" is necessary for insight to be useful or effective. Insight without ego strengthening measures sometimes leads to experiences of helplessness, fears of inadequacy and frustration. Clients with this difficulty express such things as: "I know what I'm doing, but can't seem to stop doing it", or "It doesn't seem to help me, even though I understand."

There is a story told of a person with a phobia of crossing the street. A friend suggests that he get psychoanalysis for his phobia. Years later, he saw the formerly troubled friend and inquired how he was doing, and did he ever get over his phobia? "No," answered the friend happily, "But I really understand it!"

Insight sometimes is prized and cherished, while the difficulty is thought of as merely a presenting problem. In self hypnosis, action and change are important as well. Insight may or may not be basic with all people. One client, an attractive girl in her early 20's, spent several years doing hypnotherapy to make major alterations in her personality. She went into a fairly deep trance and learned to express herself unconsciously with automatic writing. In all the time that she was involved in hypnotherapy, she never once wanted to read her automatic writing upon awakening. She changed tremendously from being shy, withdrawn, afraid of driving a car, and living at home, to pursuing school, a career, driving her own car that she enjoyed, and living on her own. This growth and development took place unconsciously without a great deal of conscious understanding, yet she enjoyed the benefits of the change.

A basic notion of Gestalt Therapy is that orientation and contact must be conscious and aware. Perls believed that awareness of the contact boundary was important for healthy adjustment in life. Confluence and the loss of contact represents a loss of boundaries between self and others which leads to neurotic functioning.

Hypnosis shows that there can also be a fine and sensitive unconscious contact with oneself and the environment. This can be very useful both therapeutically and practically. There is great ability for intelligent orientation in the unconscious. Sometimes the conscious orientation that the person has is limited and rigid. A corrective emotional experience can take place during the interpersonal interactions of therapy or be facilitated in self therapy, sometimes without conscious knowledge that it is taking place.

Whitehorn wrote of the "corrective emotional experience" in therapy. Whether this is due to desensitization and reeducation or other factors, the experience brings about therapeutic change. The patient can grow from an experience without necessarily understanding how or why it is helpful. Usually, conscious insight follows if it is necessary. The change is the most important factor. The insight may only be symbolic of the change. Many kinds of experiences may produce a corrective, therapeutic effect. This may be brought about unconsciously.

Erickson demonstrated unconscious orientation in his seminars. In one particular learning session he had been speaking for some hours, spinning a multifaceted and multitextured mosaic of teaching stories, during which many of his students had been in and out of trances when appropriate and useful. One of the women attending was quietly in a trance in her chair while he continued. All the others had come out of their trances and were watching. He quietly directed everyone's attention towards her while he subtly and indirectly encouraged her to awaken. She opened her eyes and seemed slightly disoriented at first, looking about to check out what was happening. He asked her directly what he had been talking about. She demurred that she had not been following his conversation, that she had fallen asleep or into trance. Erickson then asked her to recall what the last thing was that she remembered. Gradually he gently but confidently drew out from her an almost complete account of what he had said, beautifully illustrating how accurately though unconsciously she had been oriented. The one thing she did not recall was directly related to her psychological difficulty. He proceeded to work on it hypnotically.

David Cheek wrote on the ability of patients to be aware of what the surgeon says during operations. (Cheek, 1959, 1981) He cautioned surgeons to be reassuring and careful of what they say, since patients can pick up worries, discouragement, and negative suggestions unintentionally implanted by the mechanism of "spontaneous autosuggestion."

Erickson, guiding Rossi in how to do self hypnosis, encouraged him to experiment with becoming unaware of his body and progressively to become unaware and disoriented as to time and place until the experience of the inaccessible potential became available, e.g. a memory he could not remember, or a chronic pain that he might have to deal with. (Erickson, 1980)

Exercise: Allowing the Unconscious Response

Place your hands comfortably on your legs as you sit in a relaxed position. Think of a question which you do not have a conscious answer for but that your unconscious mind might know. For example, ask yourself if you really want to do something you have scheduled for yourself, or do you want to go into trance today, etc. Assign one hand as yes and the other as no. Then wait for the response which will be experienced as either movement, tingling, warmth, or any possible response in one hand or the other. Do not interfere consciously with the process.

You may want to experiment with automatic writing, or inviting your unconscious to "flash" a picture or word associated with the answer. Once you are able to communicate with your inner understandings, the flow of information helps you make choices in harmony with your true needs and wishes.

The Learning Task

The "task", a term used by Milton Erickson, is another way to work unconscious learnings into one's life.

Haley has written extensively on tasks as ordeals, often intending that the hypnotist remain "one-up" and the subject experience involuntarily that it is extremely uncomfortable and negative to keep on doing the behavior or indulging in the problem. The aspect of tasks that Haley found most fascinating was paradox, (Haley, 1963) in which the therapist prescribes the symptom with a minor change. In an example which Erickson described, a nail-biting child was told to bite one nail on each hand, but to leave all the rest alone. He was told to do the biting in front of his parents as loud as he liked for twenty minutes a day. The result was that once the child was ordered to do the very thing he used to do in rebellion, the satisfaction was removed. Gradually the child bit less and less until he stopped entirely.

Another use of the task is to give the client an experience in which he can grow. One client came to the authors for hypnotherapy to help him write his dissertation. He had been trying for months to write it but found that instead he was watching television for twelve hours a day and had gained 30 pounds. The harder he tried to work on the paper, the less he was able to do it. He went into a comfortable trance in the session and felt very relaxed when it was over. We asked him if he would be willing to do a task, the only requirement being that he agree to do it before he knew what it was. He said that he would. We told him to climb a mountain. He thought that was an absolutely ridiculous thing to do and had no idea how it could help but agreed to do it because he said he would. He returned several weeks later looking quite elated and much thinner. He said that after the session he was puzzled and thought to himself that there was no way climbing a mountain could possibly help him. However, he had agreed to do it, and one day when he was walking on campus he saw a hill and decided that perhaps climbing a hill would satisfy the requirements well enough. In the middle of climbing he was suddenly struck with a realization. This was exactly what he had done with his dissertation! He had always thought his dissertation would represent the culmination of his years of graduate study and would be on a certain topic which had always interested him. But when the time came he thought this would be too time consuming and opted for an easy topic which he could finish in little time. His inner self had rebelled and refused to let him "cop out." In the interim period he had changed the topic back to his original choice and began working hard every day.

This example shows how the unconscious knew exactly what the client needed to do. However, he had been unable to access this information by traditional methods. Sometimes the unconscious can help if given a situation in which it is free to make discoveries. This is the purpose of the task which is most applicable to self hypnosis. The reader is encouraged to look at the many exercises in this book as tasks, that is, learning opportunities. In an exploratory atmosphere the unconscious is usually most at home and can surprise you with helpful and practical discoveries.

There can be an inner dialogue, an interaction with your own unconscious. Listen to your unconscious while allowing your conscious mind to have its influence. The interaction between the conscious and unconscious mind, the whole person working as a unity, can bring about change. Your conscious mind can learn a great deal from your unconscious. Your unconscious can also learn independent of your conscious mind, depending upon "The personality, the situation, the reaction." (Whitehorn, 1963) This means that usual concepts, such as, "I'm totally illogical, only my intuition is accurate," or "I am incapable of anything which is not rational," must be set aside. Hopefully the exercises and theories presented in this book can help the reader to gain a mutual respect for all facets of the mind. This may lead to a deeper unifying fulfillment of the total personality. Sometimes it may even take place without rationally processing it.

Chapter 7
Creative Learning and Problem Solving

> I do not say that we should try, without training or experience, to explore our own subconscious depths. But we ought at least to admit that they exist, and that they are important, and we ought to have the humility to admit we do not know all about ourselves, that we are not experts at running our own lives. We ought to stop taking our conscious plans and decisions with such infinite seriousness.
>
> (Thomas Merton)

The mind often presents resistance to change. Sometimes the resistance may be due to conflicts and problems that are unconscious, making the defenses work overtime. Other times, these difficulties may be considered to come from conscious sets and limitations. In this chapter the reader can work with both kinds of resistances. He will learn to explore and familiarize himself with defenses and approach conflicts and problems with a more positive attitude. The reader can also experiment with bypassing conscious limitations using the unconscious in trance.

Unconscious Resistance: Opening Your Mind to Change

People often develop habitual ways of doing things. (Chapter 3) Concomitant with habit in action is habit in thought. One might notice this in carrying out a typical activity, such as washing the dinner dishes or driving the same route to work, or sitting on the bus home from work. There are certain characteristic thoughts which typically go along with the habitual activity. These habits can, at times, prevent people from growth and development.

Exercise 1

Target a specific routine activity and chronicle your thought processes for a week or so. Do not interfere with the natural flow. Simply notice it, as an onlooker watching without censure or judgment.

In previous exercises in this book, and particularly in this chapter, you are exploring areas of your inner self. Like a scientist gathering data, you are in process and do not have all the evidence collected. It is premature to draw conclusions based upon the partial information you have. Consider the next exercise as a training session for later self-therapeutic work you might do. It is drawn from Gestalt Therapy (Perls, Hefferline, Goodman, 1951) and teaches you to follow the stream of your awareness. Both conscious and unconscious skills are helpful. Hypnosis can use conscious and unconscious self suggestion. Similarly, therapeutic inroads can be made, moving from conscious to unconscious as well as unconscious to conscious, or even unconscious to unconscious.

Exercise 2

Find an undisturbed place and relax for a few moments, but do not go into trance. Instead, describe to

> *yourself what you are experiencing by beginning each sentence with, "Now I am aware of..." Though it may seem to be somewhat contrived, this exercise can clarify how your awareness might jump from e.g. a visual perception: "Now I am aware of the table in front of me" to remembering: "Now I am aware of recalling the old coffee table we gave away: to feelings: "Now I am aware of feeling uncomfortable doing this," to the future: "Now I am aware of wondering what's for dinner." (From Perls, Hefferline, Goodman, 1951: 31)*

Do this exercise several times at different sittings until you feel that you can follow your awareness somewhat. Ask yourself what difficulties you may have experienced. Has anything prevented you from successfully continuing to be aware, moment to moment? You may feel that the exercise was easy or dull. But what led you to stop when you did? Did you get to a point when you ran out of things to say? What point was it—or what areas were you ignoring? For example, some people do well with pointing out every object around them, and then they stop with nothing else to say. In this case, the individual is ignoring or avoiding his inner experiences, reactions, and associations while attending to externals, or the outer field of experience. Try to explore your own reactions to the exercise but remember not to chastise yourself for deletions. You can learn as much about your resistances by what you do not include as by what you do include. They are gaps or missing parts of your experience. Sometimes people avoid what is happening now by immersion in the past, or worry about the future. Perls's later formulation included past and future from the standpoint of the present, a more mature and realistic use of time. (Perls, 1969) All of this will be useful data in helping you to overcome difficulties or to expand potential.

Exercise 3

> *Now that you have experimented with following your awareness, choose an activity to follow which you feel*

gives you some difficulty. If you have had trouble going into trance, use this as your example. Or perhaps you feel held back in something, or have trouble relating to someone close to you. Once you have chosen a target area, let yourself recall an instance by picturing it or thinking about it. While you consider this, try to be aware of your experience. Use the previous exercise format if it is helpful.

Think about your response to this exercise. Did you have any accompanying thoughts or feelings? If so, consider possible meanings. Do you see any connection to the experience you imagined? If not, do not push it; simply allow your associations the freedom to flow wherever they tend to. Follow them without interfering while carefully observing. Sometimes these associations are peripheral and distant, almost beyond grasp. Be patient and alert to even the most minute cues. If you are touching upon a conflict area you might find that you feel nervous or uncomfortable. Rather than worrying about the nervousness, you can consider it a possible indication that you are beginning to explore something which is important. Resistances may be boring, uncomfortable, or embarrassing. You may have lost your train of thought suddenly, or have even forgotten to concentrate. Take note of this and you can learn about yourself.

Preventing Yourself from Change

If you feel no anxiety do you find instead that you are having a defensive reaction? Defenses are a way people use to cope. They are a method automatically adopted to protect against anxiety and threat. For example, instead of feeling nervous about interviewing for a new job one might feel forgetful or even draw a blank. This is one characteristic pattern of defense. A few commonly used defenses follow.

Projection occurs to deal with an unwanted emotion such as anger. Instead of feeling angry the person experiences

Creative Learning and Problem Solving

anger as coming from others. Thus a person who projects anger experiences family, friends, or society as angry at him, or annoying him. Another commonly used defense is repression. An uncomfortable or unpleasant experience is repressed or forgotten, as if it never existed. Repression is used frequently over small unpleasantries as well as major disturbing events. Rationalizing involves making a string of explanations for why one feels something. Generalization is characterized by statements like "This is a bad day" or "Everything always happens to me" or "Nothing ever goes right." The reality sense or meaning of the event tends to be obscured by this strategy.

Defenses tend to alienate a person from his inner self when overused. They may put him at a distance from his true reaction or feeling. There are times when using defenses is helpful, when feeling the full force of an experience is not appropriate. For example, during crisis the defenses are invaluable in helping people cope well. In job situations it is usually better not to tell the boss off just because one is angry. When used automatically, without any recognition, defenses may limit a person's options. Reactions become patterned too predictably to allow for creativity, excitement, or growth. This can present problems when one is trying to make personal changes, as in self hypnosis. Change is facilitated by freedom of choice.

Working with Defenses

Hypnosis is often an effective way to bypass defenses. Trance works directly with the positive unconscious and bypasses conscious ego functions like defenses. However, if you have found that you are unable to go into trance, you may be putting up defenses to trance itself. If you would like to explore this possibility, try the exercises which follow.

Exercise 1: Identifying Defenses

Think about trying to go into trance again. As you

contemplate the possibility of going into trance, what is your reaction? Do you feel vaguely uneasy and then immediately make a number of convincing excuses for not doing so, or come up with countless reasons why you couldn't? You could be rationalizing. If these excuses are highly theoretical, you may be intellectualizing. Or maybe you feel like circumstances never allow you to sit down to do a trance. Then you could be externalizing, putting responsibility outside yourself. If you believe other people try to prevent you from trance you may be projecting. Fear of trance might indicate that you are using a phobia as a defense. The insight gained from self-observation may be helpful in therapeutic efforts to change.

It is difficult to diagnose yourself just from a book, but to simply view your reaction as possibly defensive, without labeling which defense, may help you question whether this reaction is the only possible reaction you could have. People usually experience that defensive reactions are a fixed reality which always happens to them. The sense of free will or choice is not experienced. To begin to experience another possibility can be the opening wedge for new options to begin.

Exercise II

A day or more following the previous exercise, try to go into trance. This time, if you feel the usual reluctances, try to exaggerate them. If you find your attention wandering, let yourself think of anything but trance. If you feel bored, bore yourself further. After 15 or 20 minutes of this, try once again to return to trance. Some people will automatically find themselves going into trance at this point. Others will not. If not, shift back to the defense and exaggerate it further. There is much to learn from studying how you prevent yourself from successfully accomplishing your goals.

The Positivity of Negativity

Perhaps you have faithfully attempted to work your way through this book. You have sat down for exercise after exercise and found that in spite of all your efforts you cannot achieve even the slightest semblance of trance. You might feel frustrated and angry at yourself or maybe have debunked the efficacy of hypnosis. But have you ever considered the strength which is expressed in your resistance? This strength, if properly utilized can actually become a driving force in resolving difficulties. Defiance can be strength of self assertion when it matures, integrated with the whole personality.

An attractive college woman came to the authors to lose weight using hypnosis. She also complained about being very forgetful; she forgot her keys, the date, or even her best friend's name! She learned to develop a relaxing trance and was invited to allow her unconscious mind to work on these difficulties. What she discovered was that she could forget to overeat. At first, she related at a later session, she forgot several meals including her favorite desserts. She thought this must simply be an isolated incident and could not possibly related to her hypnotic work. But she continued to experience the forgetting of food and gradually began to recognize that what she had always considered to be a deficit and a problem could actually become an asset. Concomitantly, her forgetfulness with keys and other things lessened, much to her surprise!

Once the unconscious is engaged to work in a positive way problems may not merely be bypassed but instead can be used as an asset.

Exercise III

If you sense that you have some negativity which holds you back, experiment with inviting your unconscious to make some connections for you. Your unconscious may know these things even though you do not know consciously. After all, you probably did not con-

sciously choose to be negative or to have this or that difficulty. Your unconscious can change this naturally and automatically, when you allow it to do so.

During this exercise, think about some of your talents and strengths. Next, consider your weaknesses and faults. Now, relax as much as you can, going into trance if possible. Think about the human body: how the different systems are all connected, the skeletal system to the cardiovascular and muscle systems, the digestive system, etc. Consider the interactions, the overlaps. Once you have imaginatively gone through the body as best you can, relax and let your thoughts wander. Then take a few moments to pause and sense whatever your experience is like.

Bypassing Conscious Limits through Creative Problem Solving

In the first part we worked with unconscious resistance and some ego defenses. This is only one way that people prevent themselves from fully functioning. Though the conscious mind can be helpful for learning and rational thinking, it can also hamper creative problem solving. The conscious mind often prevents change and growth because of conditioning, narrow thinking, and learned limitations. In this section we will learn to bypass conscious restrictions while developing intuitive, unconscious processing.

Frames of Reference

In Erickson and Rossi's theory of hypnosis, people can accomplish things unconsciously, without interference form the conscious mind. In order for this to occur, the conscious mind is "depotentiated". One's awareness is not engaged in what the unconscious is doing. People experience this naturally when they are (for example) daydreaming.

Exercise I

How do you go from the living room to the dining room? Think of as many ways as possible. Do not read on until you have given yourself at least 5-10 minutes to ponder this. Jot down some notes on your answers.

Now analyze your responses to learn about yourself and your limitations. Erickson used this exercise frequently. He would say that he knew many ways to go from one room to the next. He could crawl, skip, run, do cartwheels, ride a bike, or roller skate. Or he could go out the door, get in his car, drive to the airport and board a plane for Hawaii. He could spend two weeks there, relaxing and enjoying the sights, then return home, get in his car and walk in the back door, through the kitchen which leads directly to the dining room.

Did you get stuck after walking, running, skipping, or crawling? Continue reading.

Exercise II

Imagine a place where there are six directions. Now think of one with two directions. Once again, do not read on until you have given yourself time to think.

There is a place in Arizona where the Cliff Dwellers lived. The terrain was so mountainous that one dweller's house could be directly above another. Thus, besides N. S. E. and W. they also had up and down, giving six directions. Now, what about two directions? Many people have been to this place. The answer is coming home on a boat. What is most important is landward or seaward. There, the compass directions are also used, but when it is late and you are tired, your main concern is landward! On boats, there is also an intrinsic orientation to the boat itself: port and starboard, towards the bow or stern, or amidships. Perhaps you know of other orientations in other contexts that are taken for granted.

Exercise III

Look at the following drawings. Can you see two images? Try to see both the faces and the vases. You can only see one of these two different images at a time. In order to shift from one image to the other you must conceive of the background differently for each. First, to see the vase, think of the two outlines and the background. Then to see the faces as the figure, think of the vase as background.

Creative Learning and Problem Solving

This example is a paradigm for how the context with which we view a situation can affect what we experience. This is particularly clear when placing a color against different backgrounds.

Exercise IV

Take a piece of dark blue colored paper and cut it into a 3" X 3" square. Place this on a red background and look at it. Next look at another blue square on a yellow background. You will see how different the two blues appear if you place the samples side by side and compare.

Perception is relative to context and perspective. People take their point of reference for granted, assuming that everyone shares the same reference or that theirs is right.

"Which Way is Right?"

A certain wise man was widely reputed to have become irrational in his presentation of facts and arguments. It was decided to test him, so that the authorities of his country could pronounce as to whether he was a danger to public order or not. On the day of the test he paraded past the courtroom mounted on a donkey, facing the donkey's rear. When the time came for him to speak for himself, he said to the judges: "When you saw me just now, which way was I facing?" The judges said: "Facing the wrong way." "You illustrate my point," He answered, "for I was facing the right way, from one point of view. It was the donkey which was facing the wrong way." (Sufi story)

A favorite joke in experimental psychology is that in which a laboratory rat says of its experimenter: " I have trained that man so that every time I press this lever, he gives me food." (Watzlawick, 1974)

Creative Thinking

DeBono has developed a theory of thinking which he defines as "The deliberate exploration of experience for a purpose." (DeBono, 1976: 32) He believes that people are usually taught to think logically: "A" follows "B" directly; one fact builds upon the next. However, logic is limiting whereas thinking is a skill which can be developed. Thinking is a skill in perception, not logic.

Most creative problem-solvers agree that there are obstacles to open thinking which can be overcome. Defining a situation too early and looking at things from a limited perspective leads to limited thinking.

DeBono's concept of "Lateral Thinking" involves a refusal to accept rigid patterns and an attempt to put things together in different ways. (DeBono, 1970: 52)

Exercise I

Combine ▲ + ▲ = ◻

Now what do you have if you combine four triangles? If you answer, two squares, think again. The answer requires a reorganization and rethinking of the shape to come up with one larger square made up of four triangles.

Similarly in working with yourself, you might develop certain patterned ways to look at situations. You may say that you have one experience and another which always seem to go together a certain way. More experiences are dismissed as simply more of the same. People often sort their experiences into restrictive, rigid categories, feeling bored or stuck. Gabriel Marcel called this, "Hardening of the categories". An open attitude towards interpretation can help.

Judgment

One of the greatest enemies to creative thinking is passing judgment, in the sense of jumping to conclusions. This is not to imply that judgments in general are unhealthy. Rather, this refers specifically to judgments in terms of personality growth and creative thinking. When dealing with personal changes it is very important to keep an open mind to the discoveries made along the way. Any conclusions are temporary rather than final.

Who Can Say If It's Good or It's Bad (Sufi story)

There was once a farmer who went to the village Master to complain about his plight. He told the Master that his farm was failing. It was too small to reap any profits and he thought everything was terrible.

The Master replied, "Who can say if it's good or it's bad."

The farmer returned to his farm somewhat puzzled. That night a wild stallion appeared on his farm. The farmer captured the stallion and harnessed it for work. A week later he returned to the Master. He told the Master how overjoyed he was that the stallion had come, for now he could plow double the fields. He took all his money and invested in seeds, expecting that at last he would make great profits.

The Master replied, "Who can say if it's good or it's bad."

The farmer returned to his farm even more puzzled than last time. He planted the seeds and worked very hard over the next weeks. The plants grew well and he looked forward to harvesting the crops soon. Then, one night the stallion disappeared. The farmer was crestfallen and returned to the Master lamenting the loss of the stallion. Now all was disaster, since he had spent his last dollar on the seeds and all the fruits and vegetables would rot without the horse to help him harvest.

The Master replied, "Who can say if it's good or it's bad."

The farmer returned to his farm feeling desolate. But the next morning, to his great surprise and joy, the stallion returned and brought with him a mare. Now the farmer was elated! Not only would he have plenty of work force from both horses, but he would also be assured of his future since there would be more horses from the pair over the years. He dashed to the Master to tell him the wonderful news.

The Master replied, "Who can say if it's good or it's bad."

The next day the farmer's eldest and strongest son was riding the stallion, harvesting the crop. Suddenly the stallion reared and threw the son off, breaking his back. Now the farmer was very upset. His son was the best worker but would have to rest in bed for months. He told the Master that his grief was boundless.

But once again, the Master replied, "Who can say if it's good or it's bad."

As it turned out, the National Army came around to all the farms recruiting the first born son of every family to battle at the front lines. Because the farmer's son was injured, he did not have to go. And who can say if this was good or bad? It is possible that the son might have gone on to become a war hero and become a stronger person from the experience, or maybe he would have been killed.

Judgments often put people on a roller coaster of emotion. The interpretation given to the circumstance can be seen from many perspectives. People will often see only the obvious which limits the possibility for positive consequences.

Choosing a Hypnotist

The reader can work with self hypnosis when he learns to voluntarily allow the involuntary to occur. The limitations and conscious objections can be set aside temporarily for the purposes of self exploration and personal growth. Ultimately, trance is a personal experience which no one else can force to be a certain way. It is possible that with time and regular attempts such individuals will be able to make the necessary discoveries for trance. If the reader finds that he still has not been able to experience hypnosis and accomplish his positive goals, it may be helpful to consult a professional. Therapeutic trance ultimately takes place within the patient, but sometimes someone who is trained to recognize and guide in hypnosis or hypnotherapy will make the difference.

Often you can accomplish your goals by working on your own, but certain problems or circumstances lend themselves to consulting a professional. You might wonder, how do I know when to consult an expert? The answer may lie within your own experience. You are obviously interested in hypnosis or you would not be reading this book. Experiment with the general exercises in trance and suggestion. If you find that you can readily experience trance or that after practice you begin to find your way into hypnosis, then you know that you do have the ability to experience self hypnosis without external guidance. If you cannot make any headway with these techniques and have worked through Chapter 7 as well, you should consult a professional to help you. This does not indicate that you cannot work with hypnosis. If the motivation is present, you will be able to experience trance with proper guidance. You may find it helpful to work with a therapist if you feel stuck or threatened, or just to help get you back on track, or to guide you in certain areas where you experience blocks or fears, or for support and help.

Choosing the right professional is an individual matter. There are a great array of professionals available: medical doctors, psychiatrists, social workers, psychologists who do hypnosis and hypnotherapists. The ideal combination is a person with experience and dedication to hypnosis as well as the helping professions. It takes both skill and professionalism: hypnosis is an art and a science.

Research supports the significant value of the therapist-patient relationship (Frank, 1973). This variable is often necessary for change when severe inner trouble is present. Self hypnosis is not intended to substitute for professional treatment, but rather to supplement or complement it.

A second consideration is the approach of the professional you choose. Learning to use your own unconscious to problem solve and make changes is central, and you should look for this to occur in hypnotherapy.

Chapter 8
Changing Paradigms

Study it extensively, inquire into it accurately, think over it carefully, sift it clearly, and practice it earnestly. When there is anything not yet studied, or studied but not yet understood, do not give up. When there is any question not yet asked, or asked but its answer not yet known, do not give up. When there is anything not yet thought over, or thought over but not yet apprehended, do not give up. When there is anything not yet sifted, or sifted but not yet clear, do not give up. When there is anything not yet practiced, or practiced but not yet earnestly, do not give up. If another man succeed by one effort, you will use a hundred efforts. If another man succeed by ten efforts, you will use a thousand efforts. If one really follows this course, though stupid, he will surely become intelligent, and though weak, will surely become strong.

(The Doctrine of the Mean,
Classic Chinese Philosophy)

Problems dealt with properly can build strength of character. William James felt that people should try to do something that is hard to do every day. If circumstance surprises you with difficulties, you are then more prepared to deal with them.

Self hypnosis can be applied to many specific problem areas. Most self hypnosis books approach it as a cookbook of recipes for specific problems. The intent of this volume is to teach the principles of unconscious functioning so that each person can individualize his own change.

Although these exercises seem to apply to one area, you may well find that they overlap with other areas of interest. Amongst all the many exercises throughout the book, you may find something that helps you. You may read about sports, or weight yet learn about many varieties of understandings that can help you with your own problems. The process of change within the self is very individual and not a symptomatic, behavioral change alone.

It is assumed that the reader has experimented with the exercises in earlier chapters and will have developed a variety of tools for inducing trance and working with the trance state. Suggestions, both direct and indirect along with experiencing in many modalities can be used to engage both the conscious and unconscious mind in the exercises which follow. The ultimate goal in all of the applications is to form a better working relationship between the conscious and unconscious mind so that a constructive multi-leveled problem-solving approach can be effective with self hypnosis. Details on going into trance are not given in this chapter since the essence of this chapter is what Erickson termed "trance utilization." If the reader has difficulty achieving a trance state, he should review the previous chapters until he can produce a comfortable trance. This chapter includes many practical applications for self hypnosis. Read and experiment as in earlier chapters. The exercises are designed as stepping stones, springboards of self-exploration and development. Let them inspire your own ideas, associations, and resources for change.

Sports: Achieving your Personal Best

Most athletes agree that sports involves more than body mechanics. The unconscious plays a significant part in performance during competition and training. Many articles are available in sports magazines instructing athletes to think positively and concentrate. These methods employ the conscious mind, and as shown earlier in the book, have their limitations. This is because the defenses, negative experiences, and narrow frames of reference that may prevent peak performance tend to interfere with change. Through hypnotic methods these learned limitations are bypassed so that untapped potential can be developed. Gains occur naturally, felt almost as if they "just happen." This is autonomous learning: evolution from the unconscious mind.

Everyone has times when he or she is "on." Irrespective of the training which went into preparation for a competition, the athlete has times when everything "clicks" and often seems to gather momentum towards peak performances throughout the contest. Compare this to another competition when the athlete feels equally well prepared, and yet inexplicably did not perform his best. Another time, perhaps, he had entered competition wishing he had at least two more weeks to prepare, then surprised himself by surpassing his personal best to date. What makes the difference in these cases? What separates the winners from losers among equally skilled participants? The martial arts has long held the answer to these questions: mind.

> Technical knowledge is not enough. One must transcend technique so that art becomes an artless art, growing out of the unconscious.
>
> (Daisetsu Suzuki, 1959)

In the exercises which follow the reader is invited to explore his conscious and unconscious mind and to experiment with allowing mind and body to function even more optimally. This is accomplished by altering obstacles to peak performance while also tapping potentials for further development.

Preliminary Exercise

Allow yourself to go into trance. You might like to drift into trance as you recall a pleasant memory or experi-

ence when you felt at ease. Relax and let your conscious mind think about whatever it likes, since your unconscious will be more important. Invite your unconscious to give you an experience in your body such as a tingling in your fingertips, followed by lightness and movement in your hand, spreading up your arm, or perhaps a comfortable warmth or heaviness. (Review Chapters IV or V if you need more guidance) As the movement or warmth or heaviness or whatever body experience the unconscious has brought about increases, you can become more curious about the exploration you are going to begin over the next days and weeks. You might wonder what it will be like to have an intuitive learning which you may or may not understand right away. Think about this without guiding your thought in any particular direction. Drift. When you are ready you can suggest that your sensations will return to normal and you can awaken relaxed and refreshed.

Pressure

Pressure in sports is one of the areas in which people consider psychological factors to be important. Pressure is not controlled by simply trying to cope through suppression. The moment that one's guard is dropped, almost anything can interfere with performance, like a snide remark from an opponent, or personal insecurities. It is better to enlist the unconscious and actually alter the meaning of the pressured situation, making it possible to grow and handle the situation with maturity.

An attractive young ballet dancer sought out hypnotherapy for her anxiety during performances and competitions. She worked out very hard when practicing, but whenever she performed her anxiety was so great that she would shake all over with tension, which she found embarrassing. She felt that performances were a tremendous pressure, with everyone's attention focused on her. She could not imagine ever being less nervous. She learned in hypnosis to relax completely and always felt relief from her symptoms following trance. A learning process was begun in trance whereby she was to put all her anxiety into her little finger, which could shake profusely throughout her performances. Of course, no one would probably notice it, but she would know. The rest of her body was free to perform her best, and she could enjoy the secret about her little finger. She reported after her next dance test that she found herself dancing well while she smiled to herself about her trembling finger. To the judges she appeared to be enjoying her performance and fully at ease, which added to her high marks. This permitted her to then explore new possibilities for herself as a performer. Only she perceived the trembling little finger.

Erickson told of a professional golfer who was hypnotized for his anxiety during golf tournaments. After treatment the man found himself approaching each hole as if it were his first. When he finished the eighteenth hole, he started to tee up again. Everyone asked him what he was doing. He said that he had obviously just started, so he was playing the first hole. He was told that he had won the tournament, much to his surprise!

In both these cases the competitors altered the meaning of the pressure in their own way: the dancer intensified and redirected the tension, thus mastering the situation. The golfer bypassed pressure altogether. In both cases, the result was to lose the usual mental concerns and self judgements along the way. The pressure can either be intensified or diminished in order to handle it. This is accomplished in an unconscious reinterpretation of the situation which allows the circumstances to be related to as they are in themselves.

Exercise

Allow yourself to go into a comfortable trance. Recall the body experience you had in the previous trance and let it develop again. Once you feel fully relaxed, ask your unconscious to think about that pressured feeling you get during competitions, performances, etc. Think about the two stories above and how these two indi-

viduals were able to alter the meaning of their pressured experience. Think about your own situation and suggest to your unconscious to make your own discovery which could change this for you. If you are involved in a sport like tennis, marksmanship, or golf which takes place over a period of time and/or points, what would it be like to approach each point, hole, or shot as if it were the first? Is there a unique way of thinking about it that frees you to be in the moment or out of context? If your sport is more of a performance-type sport such as body building, you could feel an intensification of the tension but only in your little finger or toe. Take the time to experience this fully and vividly in trance. Remember that the unconscious mind can make connections if given the chance. Set the stage for change and you may be surprised to discover new and unique solutions to your individual situation. When you are ready, wake up refreshed and alert.

Training

Nothing can substitute for good training. Getting the most out of your workouts requires more than just physical exercise. The old adage, "you get out of it what you put into it," is true to an extent. Sometimes the athlete has difficulty motivating himself to work hard between competitions. You can use your trancework to help mobilize your resources for better workouts.

Exercise

Before your next workout find a time to go into trance. Relax your body comfortably and let your mind relax as well. Think about when you felt at your peak. Remember how you felt, how your body was ready, how well you moved and performed. Remember that the unconscious mind does not understand the chrono-

Changing Paradigms

logical clock time of the conscious mind. You can recall the excitement and enthusiasm in preparing for the next work out. Let yourself relax and consider the possibilities without forcing any particular direction to your thoughts. When you are finished, wake up, relaxed and refreshed.

Motivation is important, but is very individualized: what is detrimental for one person may be very inspiring to another. For example, after the loss in one game of a series, some people get worried and tense which sends them into a downward spiral. Others seem to thrive on being behind, which triggers an intense come-back effort for the victory. For some, the desire to win when they compete can be so strong that all else is overcome. For others, taking care of certain personal needs is more central. A world champion badminton player stated that she became the best in the world out of fear: she was afraid that her opponents were training harder than she, so she worked out fourteen hours a day and put forth a continual high-pitched effort which kept her on top for many years.

Exercise:
Indirect Suggestion to Mobilize Motivation

Relax and go into trance. Allow all your muscles to relax, letting go of unnecessary tension. Suggest a feeling of warmth, heaviness, or lightness in your hand, or perhaps a certain image, or whatever you characteristically feel to be useful to orient yourself towards trance. Drift and relax for awhile. Think back to a time when you were younger and first tried to do your sport. At first it may have seemed very difficult, but can you recall how you felt about it, and found yourself wanting to be involved more and more? Recall the feelings and discovery of learning. Re-experience it and dwell on the details as vividly as possible. Relax as you think about that and then when you have considered this for as long as you want to, let yourself wake up, refreshed and alert.

Visualization or mental rehearsal can be valuable to enhance performance. Some research has shown that people can acquire as much benefit from actively imagining themselves performing their sport as from an equal amount of time spent doing it. Half of a basketball team spent practice sessions shooting baskets while the other half spent the same time visualizing themselves shooting. The visualizers did as well in a test session as the active practitioners.

Images may be visual or they can be of other senses, such as touch: you might find imagining how something feels may work better for you. Experimenting can help find this out.

Mary Lou Retton stated, when the authors questioned her at a local appearance, that she always visualizes herself doing her routines perfectly before she performs. Many bodybuilders cultivate imagery and metaphors to help them surpass their limits. Schwartzenegger liked to think of his biceps as mountains when he trained.

Warm Up Exercise: Visualization

Go into trance. When you feel ready, picture yourself doing your sport. E.g., if you are a gymnast, imagine that you are doing your routine perfectly. If you are a weight lifter, picture yourself easily lifting your limit. As a swimmer imagine yourself gliding with ease through the water faster than ever before. If a runner, imagine you are running with ease, effortlessly. Picture as many details as you can, feeling your muscles responding. Focus your attention on this and nothing else. Enjoy the feeling you get from performing your best. You might even recall a time when you actually did do well and remember clearly how that felt. Compare that imaginative experience to how you usually feel. How is this different? What did you do or feel that was unique to your peak performance?

Exercise: Indirect Visualization

Find a comfortable level of trance. Invite yourself to go even deeper, perhaps through your breathing, a sensation in your body, or maybe a hand levitation. As this continues, allow yourself to feel even more relaxed, as your unconscious responds. Have you ever been to a zoo and observed a tiger leap effortlessly across a great expanse? Or maybe you have chased your cat or dog, noting how easily your pet seems to move. Many people have watched a bird in flight, in awe of the grace. The birds fly in patterns, such as a v shape, coordinated all together. Let your mind meditate on your own spontaneous images, associations, and thoughts on this and other things. You don't know how your own associations will help you. Continue to relax deeply and absorb ideas, until you are ready to awaken refreshed and alert. Pictures or images of any sort or modality may inspire you, including music, sounds, even other sports.

Sports performance is improved by proper use of the muscles. To be able to selectively relax and contract muscles as needed can greatly improve efficiency and smoothness of performance. Many people tend to tighten all of their muscles at once when they make a supreme effort. This slows down the movements since flexibility and responsiveness are somewhat inhibited. Efficiency is reduced by this. Movement is more tiring and potentially stressful.

"Focus" in the martial arts means the relaxation followed by tensing of contributory muscles at the moment of impact. This leads to optimum speed and strength combined. You can incorporate this concept into any sport by deliberately relaxing unnecessary tensions as you practice, tensing only when necessary. Be careful not to tense unrelated muscles. In a tennis stroke, do not tighten the shoulders as you swing, or in running keep the upper body relaxed. Learning to differentiate muscle groups can be practiced on simple, isolated movement patterns. This skill can then be utilized to eradicate excessive involvement of muscles that do not actually assist in smooth, efficient use of the body for the sport.

Progressive relaxation was originated by Jacobson in his book, *Progressive Relaxation* (1929). The technique teaches the differentiation of different muscle groups leading to an overall state of full body relaxation. We will present a simplified version of the technique upon which you can elaborate further, in whatever way if most useful for you. For example, the bodybuilder might want to distinguish between the bicep and tricep. Soccer players might learn sensitive use of footwork and different parts of the foot. Martial artists might also concentrate on footwork, balance, or timed sequenced tension and relaxation of specific muscle groups.

Exercise in Progressive Relaxation to Differentiate Muscle Groups

Lie down on a comfortable couch, bed, or floor, or on the beach, or in a quiet woods; wherever you can be undisturbed. Scan your body with your awareness from top to bottom, noticing any particularly tight areas. You need not do anything about them yet. Start with your feet: tighten them as hard as you can and pay attention to the sensation. A friend may be helpful to give you feedback as you increase your contraction. Hold just your feet very tight and then relax them fully. Pay close attention to the sensation of relaxation and compare how this feels to the contraction a moment before. Try to do each phase for a minute or so. Tighten your feet a second time, then after a minute relax fully. Imagine how they felt tense and completely relaxed, noticing the differences. Next do your leg, including calf, thigh, knee, front and back, but remember not to tighten anything else, then relax. Repeat twice for each body part. Move up your body: stomach, chest, back, neck and shoulders, arms, hand, head. When you have gone through your whole body, tighten everything at once, then relax. You should feel a much greater relaxation after all. Some people find the use of a portable biofeedback machine is useful and more accurate for this, while others might prefer a friend or professional.

In general, tensions can be relaxed more fully with repeated practise.

Repeat this exercise several times over the next few days. Go back over important areas. For example, if you are a runner, try tightening your quadraceps while relaxing your calves. Or tighten your legs while you relax your shoulders and back. Imagine yourself running while you do this and keep relaxed. For weightlifters, think of a particular lift, for example, the bench press, and deliberately relax your legs, shoulders and other unrelated areas. Pay attention to the sensation of your body. There is a particular muscle set that is ideal for the bench press for you, with lower back slightly arched, ribcage expanded, shoulders back or forward; a readiness for the lift that you can feel. Tighten your chest and ready your body to do a bench press. Whatever you do, analyze your muscle patterns. This kind of work can add to your muscular control, which has subtle but certain effects on smooth performance and enhanced endurance.

For some people, especially those who have gone through the exercises in this book, specific direct suggestions can have a significant effect. Before you go into trance, think about your sport and pinpoint something you would like to improve, e.g., if you are a runner, you might like to increase your pace; weightlifters may strive to lift more weight; soccer players work on ball control and kicking accuracy. Decide upon your target. Then begin the exercise.

Exercise

Go into a comfortable, relaxed trance. Think about

your target area. Next, invite your unconscious to produce an image or a sensation to help you improve. Be willing to be open to a creative image, e.g., a runner might imagine a huge hand pushing him along, or a lightness in his legs which seems to make running effortless. A weightlifter can suggest the weight seem to be lighter than expected. Let your unconscious play with this idea even if it seems outlandish or irrational. Enjoy an overall relaxation of trance and then awaken refreshed and alert. Expect positive effects soon in your workouts or performance. Some induced suggestions may help, such as heaviness, or lightness during trance. Experiment with slowing and calming your heart rate, breathing, and other physical experiences. This control of involuntary functions can be measured. During competition the ability to be at optimum in these variables can be very useful.

The athlete who would truly excel can do so through means that transcend means, transcending technique. Technique becomes "no technique." There comes a point in which the athlete must leave behind his smaller identity and instead of expressing his ego through the sport, let the sport express itself through him. The champion bodybuilder's efforts to develop his physique, perhaps originally motivated by his ego, becomes a sculpture that tells him what needs refining. Deadly techniques of the Martial Arts practitioner paradoxically lead to his becoming peaceful yet strong. Artistry in all sports is ultimately individually motivated, yet transcends the individual's motivations as the process evolves. At a certain point the external technique must be set aside. A state of oneness takes place, in which "it" happens. As Herrigel wrote:

> This state, in which nothing definite is thought, planned, striven for, desired or expected, which aims in no particular direction and yet knows itself capable alike of the possible and the impossible, so unanswering is its power.
>
> (Herrigel, 1971: 41)

Higher levels of play can take place when no conscious thought of play is indulged in, when the focus is on permitting or allowing the process of playing the sport to be spontaneous and unintentional, without concepts, words, or labels.

A Zen master named Shoju Ronin was visited by a number of swordsmen who were desirous of improving their swordplay. His talk over tea inspired them, but they were skeptical: in the world of practical combat, they believed themselves superior. The Ronin challenged them to try to strike him with their swords, while he only used a fan to protect himself. Amazingly, they could not find an opening to attack and eventually had to admit defeat. Another monk asked how this was possible, since the master had never even practised with a sword. Shoju Ronin answered:

> When the right insight is gained and knows no obstruction, it applies to anything, including swordplay. The ordinary people are concerned with names. As soon as they hear one name a discrimination takes place in their minds. The owner of the right eye sees each object in its own light. When he sees the sword, he knows at once the way it operates. He confronts the multiplicity of things and is not confounded.
> (Suzuki, 1959: 204)

This can be applied in a practical sense to winning and losing. Takano Shigeyoshi was one of the greatest swordsmen modern Japan has produced. He states, "It goes without saying that as soon as one cherishes the thought of winning the contest or displaying one's skills in technique, swordsmanship is doomed." (Suzuki, 1959: 205)

Exercise

Close your eyes and relax. This exercise is best done sitting cross-legged and upright. Begin by following your breathing as it goes in and out. Watch each breath and eventually you will feel calmer. Next clear your mind of thoughts by imagining a blue sky, a clear still body of water, or a blank screen. As thoughts try to interfere, let them flow past without attaching yourself to them. That is, do not let yourself follow the train of that thought; simply notice it, let it pass on, and return to the image. Then, let go of the image to discover the experience of empty mind. Do this with any distraction which comes up: sounds, feelings, thoughts, and always return to the clear mind. Repeat this exercise over time and you will find that it becomes easier to do. Once you are comfortable with the exercise, try it while performing in your sport. Let your body move without deliberate thought. Maintain a clear, calm mind.

Success and expertise are developed by allowing the body and mind to act as one. Deliberate, thoughtful training of the body is done for months and months in preparation for a contest. But at the actual point of performance, the mind transcends techniques and allows the actions to flow as if automatic. This is what the Zen Buddhists call "no-mind". Thoughts or feelings do not hinder the free performance of what has been mastered, and the athlete finds himself doing his very best.

Weight Control, Impulse Control, and Regaining Positive Self Esteem

Hypnosis can be very helpful for losing weight and controlling impulses. Often the overeater is very aware that he overeats, but finds himself doing it anyway. The symptom seems to confirm the person in feeling negative. Consciously, the overeater often has an explanation for the symptom, but feels out of control. This contradiction indicates that the unconscious mind needs to be involved to get control.

Anyone who is embarking on a weight loss program and is 25 pounds overweight should double check with a physician to ensure that there are no medical problems. If no physical complications are found, it can be reassuring to know that the only obstacles to change are one's own.

The earlier chapters have covered the issue that will power is not the determining factor in hypnotic work. The impulsive person finds that the law of reversed effort from Coué will tend to override the best of intentions. It helps to enlist positive unconscious functioning to help accomplish these goals. Awareness and proper attitudes can help to set the stage to get the most benefit from unconscious work.

The dieter should begin hypnotic work on weightloss by suspending all diets to lose weight for one week. Instead of trying to cut down, attempt to eat as you normally would when not on a diet. This is not an invitation to overindulge but encourages objective observation of one's normal eating patterns. Reduce your dieting for a week. Let your natural tendencies emerge, while you watch. What happens? Remove pressures to change and notice what that is like.

Get some information on nutrition and proper diets to become highly informed about food and its effects on the body. Public libraries are a good resource. Professionals can recommend pamphlets, magazines, and books to their dieting clients. Doctors can be helpful on this; various sports or activities may have special nutritional needs as well. Consult recognized experts if necessary, to be accurate.

Not Tasting

Many dieters will say that they are overweight because they love the taste of food. However, watching an overweight person eat, one notices that they consume large quantities of food very quickly. They usually are oblivious to the taste. Learning to slow down and experience the food can be extremely helpful in overcoming weight problems. The following exercise from Frank Bruno (1972: 96-8) can help to accomplish this.

Exercise: Taste Analyzer

Choose your favorite food. Do this test when you are alone. Rate the food in terms of each of the following elements, from least (zero) to most (10)

Sweet   0 1 2 3 4 5 6 7 8 9 10

Sour   0 1 2 3 4 5 6 7 8 9 10

Bitter   0 1 2 3 4 5 6 7 8 9 10

Salty   0 1 2 3 4 5 6 7 8 9 10

Circle the appropriate number for each of the four categories. Do this for your favorite food, a food you like, and a food you dislike. Make up a taste card for each food and try many different foods. Add a brief description at the end of the taste card with the following categories: consistency, color, and appearance, temperature, and degree of liking, from 0-10.

Exercise

Go into trance. Imagine watching yourself eat, as if watching in front of a mirror. What do you notice? Try different times of the day including late night binges, early morning breakfast, for example.

Changing Habits: Analyze your eating habits. Dieters usually have a certain time of day or night when they typically indulge. For some it is a certain food which sets off the overeating. One client would eat an entire gallon of ice cream once she had a single spoonful. Another client swore that she ate no junk whatsoever, and was surprised that she continued to gain weight from healthy foods like granola, tiger's milk bars, fresh baked whole wheat bread, etc. She indulged in healthy foods: her problem was the quantity of food, not the quality.

Exercises: Eating Habits

Notice whether you eat in conflictual reaction to something, as when you are over-tired, angry, sexually aroused, or guilty. Do you have certain foods, times of day, or other triggers for your eating problem? Remember to remain objective and do not pass judgment upon yourself. You may discover that you have rational-seeming reasons for your troublesome habit.

Once you have made some discoveries about the patterns, consider the following: Do you need to act like Pavlov's dogs who always salivated when they heard a bell, once they were conditioned? If you always clean your plate, hungry or not, could you change that pattern? Being a human being with the ability to choose your actions, awareness can alter the patterns of habit if you decide to make a difference.

Other Meanings

Overeating can be symbolic of love, comfort, satisfaction, pampering, or even of conflicts and negative motivations. Sometimes, through experiences and interpretations of these experiences, a person develops a low self esteem, and feels badly about himself or perhaps feels angry at himself. Rather than feel these uncomfortable negative feelings, he develops a problem with overeating and continues to feel badly about himself now with an apparent excuse: overweight. The symptom helps to perpetuate the negative self image and so the individual becomes stuck. He might even get a secondary satisfaction by feeling sorry for himself. These patterns are often taken for granted as "the way life is" for the sufferer: trapped by circumstance. If he can work out the problems he developed from those earlier experiences and work through the negative feelings, the difficulty with weight may gradually ease. Psychotherapy or hypnotherapy can be effective means to overcome such problems, as well as interpersonal problems that relate to it as well.

Exercise:
Setting Yourself for Change with Trance

Allow yourself to go very deeply into trance. Relax comfortably. You might want to produce a pleasant sensation in your body such as a lightness all over, a warmth, or a very calm and comfortable feeling. Let your breathing become steady and calm. As you relax even more deeply, invite your mind to clear. Let yourself become calm, either through suggestion, letting go of tense muscles, or visualizing a peaceful place. As you feel the calm develop, you can begin to have confidence in your ability to relax and be calm in trance. You feel certain skills and the calm, confident feeling can increase. Let this deepen and relax fully. When you are ready, allow your sensations to gradually return to normal and wake up refreshed and alert.

Conscious insight can be helpful in uncovering self destructive patterns. Inner change must always take into account one's intuitive, non-rational side. Theodore Reik (*Listening with the Third Ear*) clearly depicts the importance of intuition as an essential component of true insight. Listen to the unconscious mind to help guide understandings of your difficulty. Ideomotor signaling can be used to communicate with the intuitive unconscious. The following trance exercise will help you to sensitize yourself to your unconscious mind.

Exercise:

Go into a deep trance. Make sure you are sitting or lying so that your hands are free to move. Assign one hand as "yes" and the other as "no". Let your thoughts drift around some of your new learnings regarding your eating problem. As you ponder this, allow yourself to go more deeply into trance. When you feel very relaxed ask whether your unconscious mind agrees with this conscious understanding. Wait for the response in one of your hands. You can check out some of your other hypotheses about yourself in this way. If you have learned and responded well, you may be able to do an automatic drawing or writing to help you develop inner rapport.

Another component of overeating is impulse control. In order to diet, a certain amount of control over impulses can be helpful. Overeaters often think that whenever they feel the desire to overeat, they are helpless to do anything about it. Trance can give a different experience.

Exercise:

Relax and go into trance. Let your muscles relax. Once you have achieved a comfortable trance state, let your mind drift, thinking about whatever draws your interest. Suggest to yourself that gradually you will develop an itch. It might be in your arm, leg, or face. As it increases in intensity, suggest that you have a corresponding inhibition to not scratch it. The more it itches, the more you will want to scratch it. But you will not scratch. After a few minutes, the itching sensation will subside, until it has totally disappeared. Some people like to relax deeply to help make the itch disappear. Others prefer a direct suggestion such as, with every breath the itch will diminish until it is completely gone. Still others discover themselves thinking of a pleasant unrelated memory and forget about the itching altogether. Experiment with different methods until you find which is most effective for you. Continue to relax in trance for a few more minutes and then wake up relaxed and refreshed.

Trance can be used to help alter a rigidly fixed self concept. The following exercise will help the dieter to accept and feel more comfortable with change.

Exercise

Invite yourself to go deeply into trance by imagining a profound sense of relaxation in your muscles. Your hands and feet may tingle and begin to feel light. The lightness in your hand can begin in your fingertips which become so light they want to raise. The feeling can move into your hand and up your arm until your whole arm raises easily. As you become more and more comfortable, feel your body becoming five pounds lighter. Enjoy how natural this feels. Continue to feel yourself getting lighter: ten pounds lighter, then fifteen, in small increments until you reach your goal. Feel this vividly and enjoy the experience. You can vary this exercise by using pictures and images instead of sensations. See yourself becoming thinner and thinner and notice how natural and comfortable this looks.

Exercise

Go into trance and try some suggestions that can make your particular weight loss easier. For example, if chocolate is your weakness, can you wonder when you will want to eat chocolate less? At times, do you forget to want chocolate? Aren't you curious what it would be like to have your unconscious help you with this? If you tend to eat at night, do you ever feel less hungry and eat less at those times? Are you ever too busy to eat, or maybe too tired? Do you have other creative ideas of your own? Invite your unconscious to use these suggestions in a positive way to help you accomplish your goals.

The unconscious mind can solve problems rapidly, intelligently, and often without conscious understanding. (Review Chapter III) Sometimes the unconscious mind knows things which the conscious mind does not yet understand. It has access to information and data beyond the senses and rational

Changing Paradigms

mind. By allowing the flow of thoughts in trance, the unconscious is freed to make connections, to learn, to develop and to change.

A young woman requested hypnotherapy for her eating problem. She worked as a check-out girl in a grocery store and complained of feeling vaguely bored with her life. She felt that working at a food store made dieting impossible. She spent her break time eating one delicious snack after another and spent much of her working time thinking about what she would be eating next. She enjoyed going into trance and found that she could relax deeply. Through unconscious exploration she discovered that in lieu of fulfilling herself in life, she was filling herself full. She was an intelligent girl who was actually interested in many areas of learning. She started to read during her breaks instead of snacking. As time went by she became less and less interested in overeating and eventually went back to school to pursue a profession.

Exercise

Go into a relaxed and comfortable trance. Ask your unconscious to review your trance learnings which you may or may not consciously remember. Think about how your body works as a unity: do you know how the bones and muscles and internal organs are all connected? You may not understand all the details of electrical theory, yet can't you turn on the light? Invite your unconscious to make connections and find solutions for you. You cannot imagine what those will be. Be willing to grow and learn if this is what is needed. You may find that your unconscious surprises you with new attitudes or different perspectives. This is only possible if you permit that inner light to shine.

When people have difficulties it is often an incomplete attempt at problem resolutions according to Rossi (1968). All of the different components of a problem are important parts of the personality, even the rejected or repressed parts. For example, tied up in repressed anger is often potential for aggression in a positive sense of action and accomplishment. An illustration of this point is the case of a woman who came to see the authors for hypnotherapy to lose weight. She was moral, kindly, and extremely religious. She often did things for others before thinking of herself. As her hypnotherapy progressed she had great waves of anger wash over her in trance. She began to recognize with time that she was very angry about many things. This put her in a bind, since she thought that expressing anger was wrong. She was not able to realize for a long time that all of the different aspects of her personality were potential assets, even if they seemed unacceptable as they initially presented themselves to her conscious mind. She needed to grow in maturity so that her anger was changed. Through trance work she was able to express many things which she never formally allowed into her conscious state. She began to integrate more and more of her inner, hidden self into her daily life in a natural way. As self acceptance took place, she found that she was less angry.

Exercise

Go into a very deep trance. Invite your unconscious to experience one of the trance phenomena you have done successfully before. Call upon the positive attitudes you have learned from trance. What is it like to accept and develop self support? Your unconscious may be supportive and helpful and you can allow this part of you to develop. As you become more comfortable with trance state and learnings, you find that you can become more comfortable with yourself and all your varied aspects. Let your thoughts drift about this and continue to relax deeply. When you are ready, awake refreshed and alert, but how long after trance can you feel more comfortable about yourself? Will you be more accepting in the morning? Or in the evening, when tired? Or when you are with friends? Or awake and alone? What potential assets do you have? Do your friends and family see more in you than you yourself do? Can you accept that you may have potential that you don't know about?

Erickson treated an overeating client by requiring that she only buy enough food for one day's meals. Each day she was to walk to the grocery store and buy only enough for one day. This demanded an absolute commitment to the process. If you are willing to do this, it is a good way to prevent the consumption of excess food and ensure adherence to a diet. Work with yourself regularly and carefully. Daily trances are best. Do not chastise yourself for slips—simply go on from there. Like the golfer who played each hole as if it were the first, you can lose one pound at a time.

Pain Control:
Expanding your Threshold for Discomfort

To most people, pain, frustration, and distress can be an uncontrollable and uncomfortable experiences which must somehow be endured until they pass. In reality, these are subjective experiences which can be controlled and altered by the individual. You have had times when you have been uncomfortable, perhaps during a flu or grief from a loss, while busy doing something else. Perhaps you were playing a competitive game or were trying to meet a deadline at work. You might not have noticed the discomfort until you stopped to rest. Then suddenly the pain surprised you and you thought of nothing else. The natural ability of the mind to disregard discomfort commonly occurs when a more compelling stimulus fills the mind. (Erickson, 1980) This subjective quality to the experience of pain makes it conducive to alteration using hypnotism.

Hypnosis has been used for pain control in numerous cases. The skills developed for pain control can be applied to psychic as well as physical pain. Recently, the authors had a client who came to learn relaxation and calming skills. She was working in a difficult marriage and outgrowing some neurotic problems but had never done hypnosis. A few evenings after her first session she phoned sounding quite distressed and uncomfortable. She said she thought that she had dysentery and had never experienced such intense pain in her whole life. Childbirth was nothing compared to this pain. She wondered if she could possibly be helped over the phone? She was told to make herself comfortable, perhaps lie down, which she did on the floor near the phone with a comforter and a pillow. We asked her to wait for response in her hands, perhaps lightness, warmth, heaviness or tingling. She felt a heaviness develop on her left side and we encouraged this feeling to spread. As we spoke to her the feeling spread throughout her left side, releasing the cramp in her intestines. It was suggested that she might like to keep a small pinpoint of pain just so that she would know what was happening and would remember to let her body heal by resting and taking the medication her doctor had given to her. She said that she would like this to happen, and so allowed her heaviness to spread everywhere except that one pinpoint of pain. By the time we hung up the phone she felt calm, ready to sleep and comfortable. She slept nine hours that night without pain or suffering. This was unusual for her, since she had been having difficulty sleeping for months.

Sometimes hypnosis can be used when heavy medication is not advised. One client had recently overcome a problem with drugs. She needed to have a nasal operation and was terrified that she might return to drugs following the surgery. She decided to try hypnosis as an alternative to medication. She learned to go into trance two days before the surgery and practiced a second time the day before. Immediately following surgery, the authors visited her in the hospital. She was in great pain and said she was very frightened. We induced a trance during which she relaxed noticeably all over. Upon awakening she felt so much relief that she even brushed her nose slightly without any pain. Several days later the authors saw her again. She stated that she had had a very strange experience. Her husband and sister had been skeptical about the hypnosis and had convinced her that all this time she was spending on relaxing and doing trance was unnecessary. Why not take a pain killer? She decided to take their advice and try the codeine pain control medication that had been prescribed. Much to her surprise and dismay, the medication did not stop the pain as effectively as hypnosis, and she was even stuck with uncomfortable side effects. She decided to recommence using self hypnosis.

Hypnosis can be a powerful analgesic whether the subject totally believes it will work or not. Hypnosis has been used successfully for control of such severe pain as that occurring with cancer patients. Barber (1980:131) states three succinct advantages for using hypnosis in cancer pain control:

1. Alleviation of pain without destructive or unpleasant side effects (Relief ranges from moderate control to total analgesia)
2. No reduction of normal functioning or mental capacity; no development of tolerance to hypnotic effect
3. Promotion of life-enhancing attitude in patients; beneficial change in attitudes toward cancer.

When used in combination with regular medical treatment, hypnosis can act as a supportive, positive adjunct for severe pain.

In some cases pain serves an important purpose, as when a child touches a hot stove and experiences the pain of a burn. Were it not for the pain receptors he might not learn the dangers of touching hot objects. Since pain serves a protective and warning purpose for the body, one must be cautious about simply obliterating all pain in all cases. However, the severity of some pains interferes with functioning and is best diminished considerably. When working with severe pain in self hypnosis it is important to coordinate with your physician or psychologist, so that you do not mask a condition you should attend to.

Methods for Pain Control

There are numerous methods of pain control which can be used. We will present a number of them with exercises and examples. Usually, one simple direct suggestion is not as effective as indirect, permissive complexes of suggestions and techniques. Experiment to find what is most useful for you.

Hypnotic Modification: This approach takes the pain

sensation and adds hypnotic sensations such as tingling, warmth, heaviness, coolness. The reader has experienced these sensations from exercises in Chapters 4 & 5. This is what was used with the woman who thought she had dysentery.

Exercise in Hypnotic Modification

Though you are highly aware of and bothered by your discomfort, you can allow yourself to relax somewhat and find as comfortable a position as possible under the circumstances. Let your hands rest comfortably and notice whether you could begin to feel an interesting sensation occur there. Let this develop into a feeling of warmth, tingling, heaviness, lightness, or whatever you would like to feel. This feeling can spread as you pay attention to it and allow it to develop. As it spreads you can feel it move over the area of discomfort, altering the experience until it is, e.g., warmer, pleasantly so, and the relaxation spreads throughout. There are a variety of possible reinterpretations. It might be warmth, or tingling, or heaviness, or feel far away. Wait to feel what it is.

Diminution: Sometimes dental pain can be extensive and intense. A young woman had undergone dental surgery and was forced the week following to either endure codine grogginess or intense pain. She opted to try hypnosis and wished to begin immediately during a party her sister was having at her house which the authors were attending. A quiet, back room was used for the induction of trance. She developed a light trance, stating that she did not feel like much was happening. She was asked to consider whether her unconscious mind knew the difference between full pain and 1% less? Such distinctions might be difficult to make, but perhaps her unconscious could make minor adjustments here and there. Her unconscious could, it was suggested, diminish the pain ever so slightly by degrees until the pain would totally disappear. She awoke from trance and said it felt a tiny bit better, but not much. Throughout the evening the authors observed her behavior change. At first she sat quietly and somewhat painfully in a corner, but gradually she began to chat here and there with people who walked by. Several hours later she was standing, smiling, and talking comfortably. When asked about her experience she stated that the pain had subsided ever so slightly at first, but after a while it was better and better until it seemed almost gone.

Exercise in Diminishing Pain

You can experiment with this kind of suggestion using trance and indirect suggestion techniques. Invite your unconscious to imaginatively compare the difference between full pain and 1% less. What is the difference between 99% pain and 95% pain? Wonder how your unconscious could lessen the pain. Would it be a gradual process of not feeling or would a different, more comfortable feeling take its place? You can wonder how long it would take to become pain-free. Allow yourself to be in trance as you think about these things. Then, awaken and allow your own unconscious to work on it in whatever mysterious way it wishes to. You do not need to know how it disappears, or where it goes.

Hypnotic Dissociation: Hypnotic dissociation has been described in general in the earlier chapters. It is possible to be freed of discomfort by watching the uncomfortable feeling from a distance. Many people have had the experience of leaving many difficulties behind to take a vacation. Upon return, the unsolved problems seem easier to handle. Erickson talked of a patient who felt faint and extreme discomfort whenever her surgeon changed the dressing. She said to her doctor,

"You know very well, Doctor, that I always faint when you start changing my dressings because I cannot endure the pain, so if you don't mind, I will go into an hypnotic trance and take my head and feet and go into the solarium and leave my body here for you to work on." When the doctor was gone she returned with her feet and head to rejoin her body, feeling quite comfortable.

(Erickson, 1980: 243)

Exercise in Dissociation

Relax and go into trance. You might want to go into trance watching yourself go into trance. You can do this by picturing yourself in trance as you imagine yourself to look. Watch as you let go of tension. See your muscles settle, your facial expression smooth out as you let go of unnecessary tensions in your mouth, jaw, around the eyes, head, neck, and shoulders. As you watch carefully you can begin to be aware of yourself watching yourself. Where are you watching from? Are you above, far away, at the beach, in the woods, watching the television or a movie of yourself in trance? Be creative and enjoy the feeling of distance. When you are ready, go back to your body and awaken relaxed and refreshed.

Exercise in Dissociation by Time

You can also dissociate in trance to a different time. In progressive illnesses it can be helpful to regress to a time when the illness was not so severe, or even before the illness began, to help feel better, and even cope better with it. This is done by working in trance with memory. Recall vividly how you felt yesterday. Remember sensations, perhaps specific thoughts and experiences which occurred. What was it like to feel pain-free? Re-experience it now. Your unconscious remembers yesterday, the day before yesterday, Thanksgiving, last Christmas, two birthdays ago, as vividly as today. Search back to a time, perhaps last summer or a particular holiday for a nice, pleasant experience you enjoyed. Vividly imagine your experience and how you were as if here and now. Use as many senses as you can imagine. Invite your unconscious to give you a full vivid memory which becomes your present experience. Sometimes this begins with a partial one. Keep this with you, a hidden resource to use whenever you need it. If the circumstances of your life demand that you face painful or uncomfortable adversity, you have resources from your own past to help you. Then, you may grow in strength of character.

Applications

Hypnosis is used for pain control in many areas such as obstetrics, dentistry, and cancer.

Obstetrics and Surgery

Childbirth and surgery can be excellent opportunities to use hypnosis. Motivation for a successful effort is very high and attention is spontaneously focused on the event. Even if you cannot use hypnosis exclusively, it can be helpful postoperatively as well. The authors used hypnosis for the birth of their second child. Practice sessions were begun during the sixth month. Hand levitation was suggested at each session, but little response was felt or observed. Meanwhile, the author continued practice sessions. She also swam daily in the bay, which she had been doing for months. The water temperature had been pleasant when she began in the summer, but as winter approached, the temperatures had dropped steadily into the 50's. Each time she swam she suggested that she would not feel cold. Much to her surprise, she felt warm and comfortable when she swam. This ability to not feel cold turned out to be useful during childbirth. Two weeks before the due date, stuck in rush hour traffic coming back from Los Angeles to San Diego, contractions began and the waterbag broke. As the contractions increased in their frequency, the authors realized that if something was not done immediately the baby might be born in the car. A relaxed trance was induced. Her unconscious mind was invited to slow down the contractions as much as possible until arrival at the hospital. The next contraction was in 16 minutes following which the contractions stopped altogether. After two more hours of driving, they stopped at home to shower, pack a bag, and leave their daughter with a friend. The authors then drove leisurely to the hospital. The doctor on duty listened to the description of events and asked skeptically, "What month are you in?" He stated that what was described was impossible but that since the water bag had broken, a bed would be prepared. At this point, the author went back into trance and a suggestion was given to begin contractions again. Childbirth proceeded calmly and normally. Whenever a contraction occurred, a hand began to tingle and raise, lowering again when the contraction was over. During delivery, the pulse rate was normal. The doctors came in following the childbirth to say how interesting the experience had been for them! They stated that the calmness was quite a contrast from the usual reaction in other patients. The author's unconscious mind had done some learning without awareness and was able to be of great assistance when the time was right.

A woman requested hypnosis for the birth of her second child nine years after her first delivery which had been intensely painful. She was terrified of the second. She began weekly sessions during the seventh month of pregnancy. She developed a deep trance and had vivid imagery of an imagined cabin in the mountains. She felt as if she was there as well as in the room with the therapist. Whenever she thought of snow, for the purposes of trance, she could put herself into a deep hypnotic state. During one of her sessions she regressed to the time of the first birth. She watched the entire process as a little mouse in the corner of the room. She noticed vivid details such as the wallpaper and the sound of the doctor's voice. She could see that although the patient was in pain, she was also experiencing the wonder and beauty of the birth experience. Upon awakening, the client remembered everything and said how she never realized that she had so many positive experiences during her first childbirth. She had only remembered the pain. She spontaneously re-educated herself to be able to have a different, more creative and positive interpretation of childbirth. The authors gave her a little stuffed mouse for the baby which she brought with her to the hospital. She reported that whenever she felt pain from a contraction she thought "Snow" and was able to delight in the birth process while being relaxed at her little cabin in the mountains.

When using hypnosis for childbirth or for surgery it is helpful to prepare ahead of time. Practice should ideally begin around the seventh month on at least a weekly basis for childbirth. When undergoing surgery, it is helpful to familiarize yourself with trance ahead of time, if possible. The subject should try many different hypnotic approaches and pay close attention to the autonomous, natural response. There is a strong motivation built into the situation which will automatically facilitate the process.

Headaches and Learning to Reduce Stress

Research over the past thirty years indicates with certainty that no single factor is responsible for causing headaches, high blood pressure, or other stress related disorders. Nor do all people react in the same way. Tension which is destructive to one person might inspire another to great accomplishments. It is always wise to first ensure that nothing is medically wrong. If this is determined to be true, then hypnosis can be used.

Erickson viewed headaches in the following way:

> Your unconscious can use a headache, use a bellyache, use constipation, use classical music, it can use a best seller, it can use a trip out to the park. Your unconscious is capable of using so many things, either for your profit or for a loss. The headache is a loss.
> (Haley, 1985: 67)

Think about stress from this perspective and change becomes easier to envision as possible. The following exercises are specifically designed for the headache or stress-prone individual.

Relaxation is one factor which can help in preventing the onslaught of a migraine syndrome, or a stress reaction. Relaxation techniques can replace chemical relaxants without any harmful side effects.

With hypnosis it is possible to be relaxed even when one is thinking about something else. As has been discussed in earlier chapters, unconscious responsiveness can occur without conscious attention. Researchers agree that certain traits can be isolated: usually people who are migraine-prone are "Intelligent, perfectionistic, ambitious, rigid, organized, cautious, and emotionally repressed." (Gould, 1973: 98) These kinds of people tend to carry a great deal of tension. Learning to overcome a tension orientation is possible and can be evoked through self hypnosis.

Relaxation: Exercise

Tense people often do not know how to relax. But, everyone has had moments, however fleeting, when they have been quite relaxed and comfortable. Perhaps it was a time with a friend, or maybe on a walk in the woods, or while curled up by the fire. Think back on a time when you felt relaxed and recall what it was like. You did not have to do or think anything in particular. You simply were relaxed and comfortable. This natural ability to be relaxed can be activated unconsciously once you have been in trance and learned to work with yourself unconsciously. Review the sections on relaxation. Work particularly on letting go of stress, allowing all your muscles to relax and be comfortable. Do not force yourself to relax. Rather, allow it to happen. Look for any small beginnings, maybe in your hand or foot, and enlarge on this response. The exercises in Chapters 4 & 5 can be helpful here. Practice them as frequently as possible until the relaxation begins to feel natural. Once you have experienced it in trance you will begin to be able to notice when you are tense during your day. Whenever possible, let go of tension in general.

Another helpful ability is hand warming. People usually find that their hands become cold when they are in the midst of tension. Warming of the extremities brings blood flow to these areas and has been shown to help reduce headache pain. Biofeedback has been used for this, as well as autogenic techniques. When hypnosis is used, no external equipment is necessary.

Exercise in Hand Warming

Lie down and develop a trance, using the hand warming exercise from Chapter 5. You may have difficulty at first producing a trance if the pain is great. However, try to focus your attention on your hands or feet. Let your body relax while you pay attention to your hands or feet. You might prefer to use an image of warmth, such as warm sun, or a direct verbal suggestion that your hands could become warmer, or a tingling followed by warmth. Experiment and refer to the earlier chapters for more ideas. Practice this several times and you will find that it becomes easier with practice. You can also experiment with hand or foot warming when you do not have a headache. Give yourself a suggestion that you will find it easy to produce the effect under any circumstances. An indirect method might be to wonder when your hands or feet will become warm: will it be now or later? You might want to use a key word or image to trigger the reaction, if you choose a consciously induced suggestion. Then allow your response to take place.

People who suffer from headaches usually have them for

a good reason. Erickson believed that an important question to ask is, how many headaches do you need for that reason, known or unknown? (Haley, 1985: 62) You might also wonder how much tension and stress is optimum for you.

Exercise

Go into trance and relax. Think about your headache or tension patterns. How long do they last? Does it really have to last as long as usual? How often, how severe, and how inconveniently do they strike? Realize that you have some unknown reason for having these headaches and wonder whether you could have less headache per month? Could your headache leave a half day sooner? Could you have those headaches more conveniently? In other words, what is the shortest, most convenient, least painful headache that will satisfy the reason. Ask yourself these same kinds of questions about stress. Let your thoughts drift and consider these ideas. When you are ready wake up relaxed and refreshed.

People who have these kinds of difficulties are often high achievers: intelligent, highly motivated people. These traits can be positive and helpful. However, there are times when one needs to find peace, to set the pressures aside, even if for a few moments. The following exercise can help to develop a comfortable image which can add to your coping mechanisms.

Exercise: Finding Peace

Permit yourself to go into trance. Imagine a peaceful place, one you have been to or can imagine going to. Envision yourself relaxed, comfortable, and totally dissociated from your characteristic pressures and problems. You might picture yourself there, hear the typical sounds, feel the relaxation in your body. Let the

> *comfort of trance spread while you enjoy the leisure of the experience. You might like to have a key word or image which can bring back the experience rapidly for next time. Think of this word now as you enjoy the serenity. When you are ready you can awaken refreshed and alert.*
>
> *Now, compare how you feel afterwards to what you felt during the positive peak in trance. What is the different sensation like? Do you discover ways to reduce stress without simply escaping your situation?*

In working with any recurring difficulty, it is important to be sensitive to yourself and your needs. To change a pattern takes time and practice. Repetition will help in time. You may or may not feel the results immediately. Hopefully, you will begin to make alterations in your typical ways of coping. You can learn to meet the challenges of life with less tension, both mentally and physically. This can have a positive effect on the headache syndrome.

Phobias, Fears, and Anxieties: Finding the Courage to Change

> Of all the emotional forces that pattern our individual and interpersonal behaviors, fear has the most insidious power to make us do what we ought not to do and leave undone what we ought to do. Under the influence, and yet trying to escape its influence, we seem fated to give it a yet stronger hold upon us.
>
> (Overstreet, 1971: 11)

Phobias and anxieties can cause great suffering and lead people to limit their lives in order to avoid the feared experience or object. They take on a symbolic significance and are accompanied by the impulse to avoid. This alters behavior seemingly against one's will.

Of all the problems which are treated by psychotherapy, behavior therapy, and hypnosis, phobias and anxieties have one of the highest success rates, with 95% being curable. People live with these discomforts, limit their lives around them, and never realize that treatment is possible.

Traditionally it has been believed that fears and anxieties derive from a traumatic event, either directly as in a near drowning causing a fear of water, or indirectly as in the classic sexual conflict which results in a fear of snakes. The traumatic episode was an early theory of hysteria. During World War II, a specific standard application of therapy used catharsis and abreaction. Hypnosis was used to reexperience the trauma of war as was described in Chapter 1. (Wolberg, 1948)

Insight alone does not always lead automatically to change. Trance work can bridge the gap between thought and action and bring about change without conscious insight at times.

An attractive middle aged woman requested hypnosis as an adjunct to her ongoing psychoanalysis to help with her phobia of driving. Whenever she got on a superhighway she was stricken with an intense panic and anxiety. The feeling was so overwhelming that she always pulled over to the side of the road. She needed to overcome this fear since her new job required that she drive on the highways. She wanted very much to be able to work at this job, but her fear was interfering. She learned to produce a fairly deep, relaxed trance. She learned about the positive potentials of her unconscious and began to feel more comfortable with her inner self.

Following the third session she reported a very strange experience. She said that she was driving in her car on the super highway and was waiting, as always, for her fear to strike. She gripped the steering wheel in anticipation, but nothing happened! She was shocked as she continued driving. She knew that she did not understand the causes or the meanings, and yet the fear seemed to be gone. She reported feeling a great deal of relief. She told her analyst what had occurred. He was incredulous. She had overcome the fear without insight! They had a series of two hour sessions to try to recover the "phobic material" because he could not accept that she could outgrow her difficulty without knowing the cause. As the reader has probably experienced, conscious insight is not always a fundamental component of hypnotic learning. At times it will occur spontaneously and naturally, and can be welcomed. Other times, the unconscious can heal itself, with a corrective emotional experience, without insight. As Perls often said, "Learning is the discovery that something is possible." (Perls, 1969: 196).

Exercise

If you are doing this exercise, you may be wondering how to become less fearful and anxious. To begin, you do not have to do anything in particular. Simply rest and allow yourself to go deeply into trance in the way which suits you best. Relax fully, let all your muscles settle, and allow your thoughts to drift. Develop a comfortable calm feeling. Trust the unconscious process. Invite your unconscious to have a pleasant memory, something you have not thought about for a long time. Perhaps you will picture the place, or maybe you will reexperience some old feelings or even enjoy listening to a familiar song. Evoke as vivid an experience as possible. When you are ready, let your sensations return to normal and wake up relaxed and refreshed.

Sometimes it is necessary to develop skills in trance which will lead to other skills. Try to develop the ability to comfortably have a memory in trance. Once this feels natural, you will be able to use this skill to help alter the phobia.

Exercise

Go into trance and become deeply relaxed. Remember that your unconscious mind can be very positive and intelligent. Things are linked, one to another, as the foot bone is connected to the ankle bone, connected to the shin bone, which is connected to the muscles, connected to the nerves, connected to the brain and so on. Let yourself reflect upon the many interrelation-

ships and interconnections between mind and body, body and behavior, mind and behavior. Now, review the significant traumatic events in your life which could be related to your difficulty. Let this happen like a dream which flashes through your mind seemingly in an instant. Consider how a child has certain learnings based upon immature thoughts and feelings which are typical to children. As a person becomes an adult, it is possible to review these experiences and reinterpret them from a more adult perspective. You need not consciously remember all the traumatic events, but your unconscious mind can reconsider the important ones from a more mature perspective, incorporating all the learnings and understandings you have gained through the years. Invite your unconscious to follow these guidelines and then wait for your responses. When you have finished, awaken refreshed and alert.

What would you be like without your anxieties? How would things change? If you suspect that you are using your fear for some other purpose and feel that you want to change, you must deal with the problem behind the fear. A woman was angry at her husband for certain personality traits he had and refused to change for her. He loved to fly airplanes as a hobby and in the early years of their marriage they flew together. But over time she developed a fear of flying. This upset her husband, but what could she do? Her phobia hurt him but she never had to feel responsible for hurting him nor did she face her angry frustrations with him. Unfortunately, her fear hurt her too, especially when they flew on commercial airlines for vacations. She suffered far more than she would have, had she dealt with the marital problems more directly. Had she recognized the link and been willing to change, she would have worked on the marriage and found the fear diminishing.

Exercise

Go into a comfortable trance. Relax all your muscles

Changing Paradigms

and let your thoughts settle. You can recall the previous trance and the many learnings you had about your phobia. Whether you consciously know them or not, ask yourself the following question. Even if you have a very good reason for your phobia, could you be without it for just one day, even one hour? Set a specific time to have a brief period of freedom from your problem and learn what you are like without it. Imagine what this will be like, and when you are ready, awaken relaxed and refreshed.

The next exercise works directly on the symptom. Some people find that this direct technique is very helpful with phobias. For others, the indirect trance work is far more effective. If you have found that you responded well to direct suggestions used in earlier chapters, try this exercise. If not, you can skip this exercise and move on. Repeat the exercise which follows, adding your own suggestions, ideas, and associations. Stimulating your own unconscious is central for success in self hypnosis.

Exercise

Go into trance. Allow your muscles to relax. Warm up with a visualization exercise. Perhaps you could picture a pleasant place, or recall the scene from a book. Relax and enjoy the image. Once you have reached a deep feeling of comfort, allow yourself to think about your fear. Begin by thinking very generally of the fear. For example, if it is a fear of water, think about water in general. Do you begin to tense as you think about it? Allow the tension to loosen by relaxing, but continue thinking about water in a distant way. Picture yourself far away from a body of water, such as the ocean, a lake, or a pool. Maintain the deep relaxation and begin to walk toward the water. The first day you may want to stop quite a distance away. Continue to relax deeply as you picture this vividly. Keep working with this image until you have successfully entered the water and remained relaxed. These learnings can be extremely helpful in altering the fearful pattern.

Repeat this exercise over several days or even weeks. Check out your reactions by thinking about water when you are not in trance and notice what you feel. You may surprise yourself. A carefully constructed hierarchy, from the least threatening to the most threatening may help you gradually face the situation and master it.

Exercise

Now that you have been working on your difficulty, you can enhance the learning that has begun. Go into trance. When you are fully relaxed, invite your unconscious to review all the related thoughts and experiences you have had. You do not need to consciously attend to all this. Ask yourself what areas need work. Be open to pursuing these findings however is best. Give yourself the following suggestions: 1) That you will work successfully on these areas 2) That you can diminish the discomfort 3) That your unconscious knows how to outgrow this and can communicate this knowledge in the ways that are best. 4) That you do not know when you will have completely outgrown the problem, but that you can learn what is necessary to learn to benefit from it.

Continuing to relax in trance, review the learnings you have had and allow the growth and development to continue. Then, wake up refreshed and alert, leaving matters to your own unconscious.

When working with yourself in any area, it is important to maintain the non-judgmental attitude which was discussed in Chapter VII. Give yourself the time you need to work on the phobia and try to be consistent in your trance sessions. When people have fears, there may be more to learn and integrate, beyond the mere symptom. If you have discovered this in your explorations with trance, heterohypnosis or psychotherapy may help to extend this learning process.

Smoking: An Example of Habit Change

People commonly go to a hypnotist to change habits. Hypnosis can be a very effective treatment since the habit is usually unconsciously motivated. People who smoke, bite their nails, or suffer from other troublesome habits, often feel that they have no control, even if they want to quit. You can experiment with the exercises which follow and invite your unconscious mind to have learnings which could be helpful for you.

People think that the first step in giving up smoking is to make up your mind to quit. The smoker must make the decision. No one can decide for him. A decision is usually not enough to make the difference except in certain types of individuals. More often, the law of reversed effort takes place. The more the smoker tries not to smoke, paradoxically, the more he wants to smoke. He becomes overcome with thoughts about smoking and eventually goes back to it. Hypnosis bypasses this process to facilitate the change.

A client came to us to quit smoking, but knew that she would have great difficulty doing it. She had failed many times before. She always gave in to the craving. We led her to a beautiful area of the ocean. She got out of the car, following, puzzled. We took a number of deep, pleasant breaths of the fresh sea air. She did the same. Then, we asked her to take her cigarettes and throw the whole package into the smelliest, dirtiest garbage can we could find, filled with vomit, dog manure, rotten food, and other choice tidbits. She told us she might return to get them. We told her she had better dump her ashtray as well. We enjoined her to memorize the smell and appearance of that disgusting garbage can, and remember that, if she felt tempted to smoke. She quit that day, never to return to cigarettes. She followed up the session about a week later with one more, to learn to relax at will. She was shocked that she had lost her craving to smoke. She did need to learn to relax at will and did so with trance.

Exercise

Read and study as much as you can about the hazards of smoking. Learn what it actually does to your lungs and body, how destructive it can be to your health. Consider how much money you spend on it and what you could do with the money you will save in not smoking. List all of the other reasons for not smoking: the unpleasant odor, perhaps others close to you who are bothered by it. There are movies available which show the horrors of a cancerous lung, slow death from emphysema, etc. These can be helpful in re-education. Your school, library, or even family doctor's office may have visual aids available as well. Becoming informed may help you reinforce a decision to quit, if that is your choice.

It can be helpful to uncover your motivations for smoking. A young woman in her early twenties wanted to quit smoking. She told us how bad it was for her health and how she knew she had to quit. She was looking forward to hypnosis and went into a deep trance. But midway through the trance she awoke with a jolt and said, "I don't want to do this!"

She explored what this meant and began to recognize that cigarette smoking gave her an excuse to sit down and rest, to do nothing but enjoy the cigarette and calm. She felt that to give up smoking meant to give up relaxing. Whenever she had tried quitting before, she always got to a point where she became so frazzled and distraught that she could not stand it, and broke down to have a cigarette. Her motivation to smoke was actually a very positive one: to relax. She had to learn to separate out the relaxation from the smoking.

People often endow cigarettes with all kinds of meanings which they do not have. A popular conception is that cigarettes are relaxing. In reality, nicotine does not relax the muscles. Instead, it has a stimulant effect. Smoking becomes symbolic for relaxation in the mind of the smoker. It is a form of auto-suggestion which gives cigarettes their seemingly powerful effect. We have often told our clients, "You were not born smoking a cigarette. You knew how to relax as a baby and you can be comfortable without them. Whatever cigarettes do for you, you can do for yourself without them."

Exercise

Trance can be helpful in making discoveries. Find a comfortable level of trance, relaxing your muscles and letting yourself have a comfortable body experience. As you go deeper into trance, imagine a beautiful, inspiring scene in nature: it might be a clear sky, clear air, the smell of fresh pine trees, or a beautiful garden, the mountains, or the ocean salt air. Breathe deeply and enjoy the feeling of clean air in your lungs. Relax and let your trance deepen. Your mind will associate to images, experiences, and feelings which are important. Your unconscious already knows what is relevant far better than you can imagine. You may have an unconscious corrective experience, without even knowing it. Or then again, perhaps you will know it. If you attempt to anticipate or preprogram what you will discover, you may miss out on many interesting new learnings. When you are ready, awaken fully alert.

Another area to explore is the habit level. Sometimes people keep smoking just because they always have. They may think themselves into a corner to justify the habit. Habit develops inertia, or the tendency for a habit already in effect to continue as before. Smokers are often discouraged and despair of change. They make an effort, fail, and then confirm themselves in a self-diagnosis, "Compulsive Smoker, Incurable". These learned limitations can be bypassed by the unconscious mind.

One of our clients wanted to quit smoking, and came for several sessions of hypnosis. We encouraged him to relax and be open to the creative potential of his trance experience. We suggested that he could make new and surprising, enjoyable discoveries before the next session, and to have some fun with it. He came to the next session smiling. He reported that he had had a surprisingly wonderful time going out dancing with a girl the night before the session. He had gone to a disco and danced so well that everyone clapped. He told us with much embarrassment that the only trouble was he did not go out with girls (he was comfortably adjusted in the gay lifestyle) and he did not know how to dance! Some months later he got in touch to tell us that not only did he still not smoke, but that he had taken up entering dance contests and was winning. Furthermore, he had discovered that he had talent as an excellent gourmet cook! His natural talents were freed from his rigid framework of habit. He evolved in new, unexpected and positive directions, stemming from his experiences in trance.

Exercise

Explore your habit. Look at how you smoke: do you use your right hand or left hand? How do you light the match? Pay attention to the automatic process of smoking. Do you feel more sophisticated? Are you at ease with a cigarette and awkward without it? Try to become fully conscious and aware of what you usually do automatically. Attention to minute detail is helpful in accomplishing this. Take about a week to work on these exercises and ready yourself to stop smoking. Think about it, explore it, mobilize your energies toward the goal, but do not stop smoking yet. You are not ready.

The following exercise should be done at the end of the conscious exploration period. Repeat this exercise several times, allowing your unconscious to explore the areas most central to your development.

Exercise

Take your time. Go into a very deep trance. Relax and

use any approach to trance which you find most effective. Deepen your trance several times, relax more with each suggestion, until you are deeper than you have ever been. Remember, levels vary with individuals and your unconscious will help you find an adequate depth for you.

Can you experimentally produce several different hypnotic effects? Try lightness, warmth, or heaviness of a limb with a nice image, or slowed experience of time, whatever you enjoy doing in trance. You know that you have begun to set yourself to give up smoking. Experiment with altering your awareness.

Have you ever forgotten that you lit a cigarette and lit a second? Have you ever thought you had one last pack of cigarettes only to find that there were none in the house? Each exercise you do in trance can be helpful in enlisting your unconscious mind to assist you in quitting. Just as your hand moves, seemingly by itself, or your body becomes heavy, so you can find that the physical "craving" you usually feel for cigarettes can be altered and dissipate. The spontaneous occurrence of an hallucination in trance can facilitate a new self image of smoking for you. Perceptions can be altered through trance. This can help you to change your emotional need for smoking. You might enjoy a new insight about cigarettes.

The unconscious gives an inner involuntary strength, adding to conscious conviction. You can find new reservoirs of confidence to help you. The discovery of your own untapped inner strength becomes the source of change. Explore your reactions to positive suggestions: can you imagine giving up cigarettes with little or no discomfort? Your body knows how to not notice many experiences and sensations. You can be calm, using hypnosis when needed, if you are willing to use your unconscious to help. The urge to smoke can be farther and farther away from linking to actually picking up a cigarette, lighting it, and inhaling.

Imagine how you would be as a non-smoker, what a positive sense of accomplishment you will have achieved. You may wonder why you did not stop sooner. What thoughts and images do you have about smoking? Your own thoughts and associations can be the source of change.

Then relax and rest in trance. Wake up relaxed and refreshed. Repeat this trance as many times as needed over the next several days. You might want to emphasize one aspect more than another at each sitting. Some will find the results are immediate while others might find that several sessions are required. When you feel ready, you can rid your house and car of all cigarettes and never smoke again.

Conclusion

The relationship between yourself and your unconscious can grow and develop in beneficial ways if you work on it. As the river flows to the ocean and becomes one with it, your intent to resolve your problems can lead you to open the lines of communications between your conscious and unconscious mind. The approach which we have presented works with unconscious resources and teaches people to be receptive to these and hopefully integrate them into their lives. People have many potentials which are often kept in reserve. As one learns to be more sensitive to the unconscious mind through trance, it becomes possible to develop one's potential in areas other than the target area only. This often occurs as a pleasant surprise. We hope the reader can apply the learnings he has gained to accomplish his goals and beyond.

Bibliography

Bakan, P. "Hypnotizability, Laterality of Eye Movements and Functional Brain Asymmetry," *Perceptual and Motor Skills*. 28 (1969): 927-32

Bandler, R. and Grinder, J. *Patterns of the Hypnotic Techniques Milton H. Erickson, Vol. 1.* Cupertino, Calif.: Meta, 1975.

___, and ___. *The Structure of Magic, Vol. 1.* Palo Alto, Calif.: Science & Behavior Books, 1975.

___, and ___. *The Structure of Magic, Vol. 2.* Palo Alto, Calif.: Science & Behavior Books, 1976.

___, and ___. *Trance Formations: Neurolinguistic Programming and the Structure of Hypnosis.* Moab, Utah: Real People Press, 1981.

Barber, T. "Hypnosis, Suggestions, and Psychosomatic Phenomena: A New Look From the Standpoint of Recent Experimental Studies." *American Society of Clinical Hypnosis*, Vol. 21, No. 1, July, 1978.

Barber, T. Spanos, N., and Chaves, J. *Hypnosis, Imagination and Human Potentialities.* New York: Pergamon, 1974.

Bassin, R. "Consciousness and the Unconscious." *A Handbook of Contemporary Psychology.* Ed. M. Cole and I. Maltzman. New York: Basic Books, 1969.

Baudouin, C. *Suggestion and Autosuggestion.* New York: Bodd, Mead, and Co., 1921.

Benson, H. *The Relaxation Response.* New York: Avon Press, 1975.

___. *The Mind/Body Effect.* New York: Simon & Schuster, 1979.

Beahrs, J.O. *Unity and Multiplicity: Multi-level Consciousness of Self in Hypnosis., Psychiatric Disorder and Mental Health.* New York: Brunner/Mazel, 1982.

Berne, E. *Intuition and Ego States.* San Francisco: TA Press, 1977.

Bernheim, H. *Hypnosis and Suggestion in Psychotherapy.* New York: Jason Aronson, 1973.

Binet, A., and Feré, C. *Animal Magnetism.* New York: D. Appleton, 1888.

Blakeslee, T. R. *The Right Brain.* New York: Berkley Press, 1983.

Bogen, J. "The Other Side of the Brain: An Appositional Mind." *The Nature of Human Consciousness.* Ed. R. Ornstein. San Francisco: W.W. Freeman, 1973.

Boring, E. *A History of Experimental Psychology.* Englewood Cliffs, N.J.: Prentice Hall, 1950.

Braid, J. *Braid on Hypnotism.* New York: Julian Press, 1960.

Bramwell, J.M. *Hypnotism, Its History, Practice, and Theory.* London: Grant Richards, 1903.

Breuer, J., and Freud, S. *Studies on Hysteria*. New York: Basic Books, 1957.

Brooks, Charles V.W., *Sensory Awareness*. Santa Barbara: Ross-Erickson Pub., 1982

Bruno, F. *Think Yourself Thin*. New York: Barnes & Noble, 1972.

Burke, K. *A Rhetoric of Motives*. Berkeley, U. of Calif. Press, 1969.

Cannon, W.B. *The Wisdom of the Body*. New York: W.W. Norton, 1963.

Carroll, John B., ed. *Language, Thought, and Reality: Selected Writings of Benjamin Lee Whorf*. The M.I.T. Press Cambridge, Mass: 1956.

Cheek, D. "Unconscious Perception of Meaningful Sounds during Surgical Anaesthesia as Revealed Under Hypnosis." *American Journal of Clinical Hypnosis*, 1, 101-113, 1959.

———. "Awareness of Meaningful Sounds Under Anaesthesia: Considerations and a Review of the Literature." *Theoretical and Clinical Aspects of Hypnosis*. Symposium Specialists, Miami, Florida, 1959-1979.

Cooper, L.F., and Erickson, M.H. Time Distortion in Hypnosis: *An Experimental and Clinical Investigation*. New York: Irvington, 1982.

Coué, E. *How to Practice Suggestion and Autosuggestion*. New York: American Library Service, 1923.

Crutchfield, R.S. & Krech, D. *Theory and Problems of Social Psychology*. N.Y.: McGraw-Hill, 1948.

Darnton, R. *Mesmerism*. New York: Shocken Books, 1970.

DeBono, E. *Lateral Thinking.* New York: Harper Colophon Books, 1973.

___. *Teaching Thinking.* London: Temple Smith, 1976.

Dorus, Roy M. *Hypnosis and Its Therapeutic Applications.* N.Y.: McGraw Hill, 1956.

___. and Shaffer, Wilson G., *Textbook of Abnormal Psychology* Baltimore: Williams and Wilkins Co., 1945

Diamond, M.J. "Issues and Methods for Modifying Responsivity to Hypnosis." in *Annals of the New York Academy of Sciences.* New York: 1974: 296, 119-128.

Erickson, M.H. "Further Techniques of Hypnosis: Utilization Techniques." *American Journal of Clinical Hypnosis,* 2, 1959: 3-21.

___. "Initial Experiments Investigating the Nature of Hypnosis.: *American Journal of Clinical Hypnosis,* 7, 1964: 152-62.

___. *Mind-Body Communications in Hypnosis.* N.Y.: Irvington, 1986.

___, and Rossi, E. *Hypnotherapy.* New York: Irvington, 1979.

___, and ___. Experiencing Hypnosis: *Therapeutic Approaches to Altered States.* New York: Irvington, 1981.

___, and ___. *The Collected Papers of Milton H. Erickson.* 4 vols. New York: Irvington, 1980.

___, ___, and Rossi, S. *Hypnotic Realities.* New York: Irvington, 1976.

Fisher, Seymour, *Body Experience in Fantasy & Behavior.* New York: Appleton-Century-Crofts, 1970

Bibliography

Frank, J.D. *Persuasion and Healing.* New York: Shocken Books, 1973.

___. *Psychotherapy and the Human Predicament.* New York: Shocken Books, 1978.

___, Hoehn-Saric, R., and Gurland, B. "Focused Attitude Change in Neurotic Patients." *Journal of Nervous and Mental Disease.* 147, no. 2, 1968: 124-33.

___, et. al. "Attitude Change and Attribution of Arousal in Psychotherapy," *Effective Ingredients of Successful Psychotherapy.* New York: Brunner/Mazel, 1978.

___, et. al. *Effective Ingredients of Successful Psychotherapy.* New York: Brunner/Mazel, 1978.

Gardner, H. *The Shattered Mind.* New York: Vintage Books, 1976.

Gazzaniga, M. "The Split Brain in Man." *In the Nature of Human Consciousness.* Ed. R. Ornstein. San Francisco: W.H. Freeman, 1973.

___, and LeDoux, J.E. *The Integrated Mind.* New York: Plenum Press, 1978.

Gurwitsch, A. *Studies in Phenomenology and Psychology.* Evanston: Northwestern U. Press, 1966.

Gould, Heywood. *Headaches: Causes, Treatment, and Prevention.* New York: Barnes & Noble Books, 1973.

Guthrie, E.R. *The Psychology of Human Conflict.* New York: Harper, 1935.

Haley, J. *Strategies of Psychotherapy.* New York: Grune & Stratton, 1967.

___. *Conversations with Milton H. Erickson*. Vol. I New York: W.W. Norton, 1985.

___. *Advanced Techniques of Hypnosis and Therapy: Selected Papers of Milton H. Erickson*, M.D. New York: Grune & Stratton, 1967.

___. *Uncommon Therapy*. New York: W.W. Norton, 1973.

Herrigel, Eugen. *Zen in the Art of Archery*. New York: Vintage Books, 1971.

Hilgard, E.R. *Hypnotic Susceptibility*. New York: Harcourt Brace Jovanovich, 1968.

___. *Divided Consciousness: Multiple Controls in Human Thought and Action*. New York: John Wiley & Sons, 1977.

___, and Hilgard, J.R. *Hypnosis in the Relief of Pain*, Los Altos, Calif., William Kaufman, 1975.

Hilgard, J.R. Personality and Hypnosis: *A Study of Imaginative Involvement*. Chicago: University of Chicago Press, 1970.

Hinkle, Lawrence E., "The Concept of Stress in the Biological and Social Sciences." *Science, Medicine and Man* Vol. I, 1973, 31-48.

Hull, C. *Hypnosis and Suggestibility*. New York: Appleton, Century, Crofts, 1968.

Husserl, E. *The Idea of Phenomenology*. The Hague: Martinus Nijhoff, 1964.

Jacobson, Edmund, *Progressive Relaxation:* Chicago: University of Chicago Press, 1929.

James, W. *The Principles of Psychology*. Vol. I & II. New York: Henry Holt & Co., 1896.

Bibliography

Janet, P. *Psychological Healing*, Vol. I & II. New York: McMillan, 1925.

Jourard, S. *Disclosing Man to Himself*. New York: Van Nostrand, Reinhold, 1968.

___. *The Transparent Self*. New York: Van Nostrand, Reinhold, 1971.

Jung, C.G. *The Structure and Dynamics of the Psyche*. Vol. 8. *In the Collected Works of C.G. Jung*. Princeton, N.J.: PrincetonU. Press, 1981.

Kline, M.V. *Freud and Hypnosis: The Interaction of Psychodynamics and Hypnosis*. New York: The Julian Press, 1958.

Kimura, D. "The Asymmetry of the Human Brain." *Recent Progress in Perception*. Ed. R. Held and W. Richards. San Francisco: W.H. Freeman, 1976.

Kroger, W. *Clinical and Experimental Hypnosis*. Philadelphia: J.B. Lippincott, 1977.

Kubie, L. *Neurotic Distortion of the Creative Process*. New York: Noonday Press, 1975.

Lazarus, R.S., and Shaffer, G.W. *Fundamental Concepts in Clinical Psychology*. New York: McGraw-Hill, 1952.

LeCron, L. *Self Hypnotism: The Technique and its Use in Daily Living*. Englewood Cliffs, N.J., 1964.

Lipowski, Z.J., Lipsitt, Don R., Whybrow, Peter C. *Psychosomatic Medicine*. New York: Oxford University Press, 1977.

Lozanov, G. *Suggestology & Outlines of Suggestopedy*, New York: Gordon & Breach, 1977.

Luria, A.R. "The Brain and Conscious Experience." *British Journal of Philosophy*, 58, 1967: 467-76.

Maltz, M. *Psychocybernetics*, N. Hollywood, Calif.: Wilshire Book Co., 1960.

Marcel, Gabriel. *Mystery of Being*. Chicago: Henry Reginery Co., 1969.

Montessori, M. *The Montessori Method by Maria Montessori*, New York: Schocken Books, 1964.

Munro, H.S. *Handbook of Suggestive Therapeutics, Applied Hypnotism*, Psychic Science. St. Louis: C.V. Mosby Co., 1911.

Natadze, R.G. "Experimental Foundations of Uznadze's Theory of Set." *A Handbook of Contemporary Psychology*, E.M. Cole. New York: Basic Books, 1969.

Nebes, R. "Man's So-Called Minor Hemisphere." *The Human Brain*. Ed. M.C. Wittrock. Englewood Cliffs, N.J.: Prentice-Hall, 1977.

Orne, M. "A Note on the Occurrences of Hypnosis Without Conscious Content. *International Journal of Clinical and Experimental Hypnosis*. Vol. XII, No. 2, April, 1964.

Osborn, A.F. *Applied Imagination, Principles and Procedures of Creative Thinking*. New York: Charles Scribner's Sons, 1953.

Overstreet, H.A. *About Ourselves*. Great Britain: Butler & Tanner, 1938.

Owen, A.R.G. *Hysteria, Hypnosis, & Healing: The Work of J.M. Charcot*. London: Dennis Dobson, 1971.

Pavlov, I.P. *Conditioned Reflexes: An Investigation of the Physiological Activity of the Cerebral Cortex*. New York: Dover, 1960.

Perls, F. *Gestalt Therapy Verbatim*. Lafayette, Calif.: Real People Press, 1969.

___. Hefferline, R. and Goodman, P. *Gestalt Therapy*, N.Y.: Dell Publishers, 1951.

Platinov, K. *The Word as a Physiological and Therapeutic Factor*. Moscow: Foreign Languages Publishing House, 1959.

Prince, M. *Psychotherapeutics*. Boston: The Gorham Press, 1912.

Pulos, Lee, "Mesmerism Revisited: The Effectivensss of Esdaile's Techniques in the Production of Deep Hypnosis and Total Body Hypnoanaesthesia," *American Journal of Clinical Hypnosis*, Vol. 22, No. 4, Apr 1980, 206-211.

Raudsepp, E. *Creative Growth Games*. New York: Jove, 1977.

___. *More Creative Growth Games*. New York: G.P. Putnam's Sons, 1980.

Reik, Theodore. *Listening With the Third Ear*. New York: Jove Publications, Inc., 1948.

Rosen, E. *My Voice Will Go With You: The Teaching Tales of Milton H. Erickson*. New York: W.W. Norton, 1982.

Rossi, E. *Dreams and Growth of Personality*. New York: Pergamon Press, 1972.

___. *The Psychobiology of Mind-Body Healing*, N.Y.: W.W. Norton & Co., 1986.

___. "The Cerebral Hemispheres in Analytic Psychology." *Journal of Analytic Psychology*, 22, 1977: 32-51.

___. "The Breakout Heuristic," *Journal of Humanistic Psychology*, 1968, Vol. 8, 16-28.

___. "Hypnosis and Ultradian Cycles: A New State(s) Theory of Hypnosis." *American Journal of Clinical Hypnosis*, 25, No. 1, 1982: 21-31.

___. Cheek, David B. *Mind Body Therapy*, N.Y.: W.W. Norton & Co., 1988.

Sarbin, T.R. "Contributions to Role-Taking Theory." I. *Hypnotic Behavior. Psychol. Rev.*, 5, 1950: 255-290.

Seyle, H. *Stress Without Distress*. New York: Signet Books, 1974.

Sidis, B. *The Psychology of Suggestion*. New York: D. Appleton, 1899.

Sluzki, C., and Ransom, D. *Double Bind: The Foundation of the Communicational Approach to the Family*. New York: Grune & Stratton, 1976.

Springer, S., and Deutsch, G. *Left Brain, Right Brain*. San Francisco: W.H. Freeman, 1981.

Suzuki, Daisetz T., *Zen and Japanese Culture*. Princeton, N.J.: Princeton University Press, 1959.

Taylor, Eugene, *Willian James on Exceptional Mental States*, N.Y.: Charles Scribner's & Sons, 1982

Thorndike, Edward L., *Human Learning*, Cambridge: M.I.T. Press, 1977.

Watts, A. *The Way of Zen*. New York: Vintage Books, 1957.

Watzlawick, Paul, Weakland, John, and Fisch, Richard. *Change*, N.Y.: W.W. Norton & Co., 1974

Weitzenhoffer, A. *General Techniques of Hypnotism*. New York: Grune & Stratton, 1957.

Bibliography

___. *The Practice of Hypnotism,* Vol. I & Vol. II: N.Y., John Wiley and Sons, 1989.

___. "Hypnotic Susceptibility Revisited," *American Journal of Clinical Hypnosis.* Vol. 22, No. 3, 1980: 130-146.

Whitehorn, J. "The Concept of Meaning and Cause in Psychodynamics." *American Journal of Psychiatry,* 104, 1944: 289.

___. "Stress and Emotional Health," *The American Journal of Psychiatry,* Vol. 112, No. 10, Apr. 1956.

___. "The Person, the Situation, and the Reaction: Psychotherapeutic Strategy." *Acta Medical Scaninavia* Supp., 196, 1947: 626-33.

Wolberg, L. *Medical Hypnosis,* Vol. I & II. New York: Grune & Stratton, 1948.

___. *Hypnoanalysis.* New York: Grune & Stratton, 1964.

___. *Techniques of Psychotherapy.* Vol. I & II. New York: Grune & Stratton, 1977.

Wolff, H., *Proceedings of the Association for Research in Nervous and Mental Disease,* Baltimore: Williams & Wilkins, 1950.

Zeig, J. A *Teaching Seminar with Milton H. Erickson.* New York: Brunner/Mazel, 1980.

___. *Ericksonian Approaches to Hypnosis and Psychotherapy.* New York: Brunner/Mazel, 1982.

Author Index

Bandler, 101-103
Barber, 25, 177
Bateson, 33, 34, 123, 125
Baudouin, 12-14
Bellak, 60, 61
Benson, 84
Berne, 67-68
Bernheim, 9-10, 14, 44
Bertrand, 4
Bessel, 80
Binet, 11
Blakeslee, 71-73
Boring, 81
Braid, 5-6, 11, 42, 48
Bramwell, 19
Breuer, 14-15
Brooks, 39, 89-90
Bruno, 167
Burke, 75-76
Charcot, 8, 14
Cheek, 133
Coe, 24
Cooper, 115-116
Coué, 11-12
Crutchfield, 45
De Bono, 148
Descartes, 79

Erickson, 26-33, 35, 37, 46-55, 57-58, 62, 63, 91-91, 105-106, 115-116, 125, 127, 131, 134, 157, 175
Esdaile, 7
Abbé Faria, 4
Fechner, 61, 81
Feré, 11
Fisher, 94-95
Frank 29, 39, 44, 73-74, 81-82, 83, 84, 124, 128
Freud, 14-15, 93, 123
Gardner, 69-73
Gazzaniga & Le Doux, 70-73
Grinder, 191-103
Gurwitsch, 74-75
Guthrie, 123, 128
Haley, 33-36, 134
Helmholtz, 80
Herrigel, 164
Hilgard, 22-23, 122
Hinkle, 83
Hull, 20-21, 26
Husserl, 63, 74-75, 130
James, 17-18, 63-65, 153
Janet, 15-17, 23

Jourard, 97
Jung, 69
Kretch, 45
Kroger, 103
Kubie, 30, 60, 63
Lazarus, 83-84
Linder, 19-20
Lowen, 90-91
Liébeault, 9
Marcel, 148
Marquis de Puysegur, 3
Maskelyne, 80
Mesmer, 2-6
Montessori, 122
Moreno, 50
Munro, 18, 19
Nebes, 71
Noizet, 4
Orne, 24
Pavlov, 21-22, 123-124
Perls, 85-89, 93, 94, 121, 132, 138-139, 189
Prince, 66
Pulos, 11
Reik, 170
Richter, 84
Rossi, 28-33, 46-55, 91, 105-106, 125, 131, 133, 173
Sarbin, 24
Selver, 89-90
Selye, 82-83
Shaffer, 25-26, 93
Sidis, 15, 17, 46-48
Smale, 83
Sperry, 70
Suzuki, 155, 165
Thorndike, 125
Uznadze, 61-62
Watts, 62
Watzlawick, 147

Weitzenhoffer, 26, 45
Whitehorn, 80-81, 132-133, 136
Whorf, 75-76
Wolberg, 15, 20, 131, 188
Zaner, 63
Zeig, 66

Subject Index

acceptance set, 51, 62
amnesia, 119, 171, 172
anaesthesia, 112-114
analytical learning theory, 124-125
animist, 6
anxiety, 187-193
association, 17-18, 50, 51, 63-65, 100-101, 123, 195
assumptions, 73, 76
assumptive world, 73, 74, 75
athletics, 154-166
attention, 5-6, 29-30, 42-43, 48, 85, 88, 94, 99, 100, 105, 107, 108, 114, 184, 192
automatic writing, 133-134, 171
awareness
  -of body sensations, 85, 88, 89-90, 94, 99-100, 107
  -of needs and tensions, 85, 87, 124, 159
body focusing, 86, 160-164
body image, 94-95, 106-108, 172

body therapies, 90-91
catelepsy, 67
catharsis, 94
coolness, sensations, 178
concentration, 85
conscious limits 144-151
conscious-unconscious balance, xviii, 68-69, 131-133
context, 44, 122-127, 146-147
corrective emotional experience, 132-133, 195
creative learning, 30, 137-150
creative moments, 30, 173
creative problem solving, 144-147, 148, 172-177
defenses, 85, 140-144, 155
demoralization, 84
desensitization, 127-129
dissociation, 15-18, 22-23, 85, 113-114, 158, 179-181, 191-192
dreams, 65-67
dualism, 79

emotions-
  anger, 173-174, 190
  and tension, 184
expectancy, 11, 27, 29, 42, 44-45, 51, 73-74, 80, 81-82, 84, 104, 124, 128
fears, 124, 187-193
fixation of attention, 5-6, 29-30, 42-43, 44
fluidists, 6
frame of reference, 125-127, 144-146, 155
generalization, 122-123
Gestalt therapy, 50, 85-89, 132, 138
habits, 59-60, 64, 168-169, 193-197
hallucination, 91, 110-112, 173, 195
hand levitation, 35, 67, 108-110, 181-197
hand warming, 109, 155, 185-187, 197
headaches, 39, 85, 183-187
hemisphericity, 69-73
homeostasis, 87
hyperaesthesia, 112, 114-115, 171, 176
hypnoanalysis, 19-20
hypnotic modification, 178-180
ideomotor, xviii, 44, 54, 91-94, 104-105, 170-171
incidental learning, 122
imagination, 50
indirect hypnotherapy, 26-36, 48-55
impulse control, 166-167, 171-173
insight, 188, 189

intuition, 50, 67-69, 71, 86, 88-89, 156, 170
judgement, 149-150, 157
language, 75-76
lateral thinking, 148
law of auxiliary emotion, 13
law of concentrated attention, 12-13
law of reversed effort, 13, 167
learned limitations, 76, 144
learning-for-oneself, 97, 128, 158
learning theories, 121-131
lebenswelt, 74-75
left brain, 69-73
magnetism, 2-6
mastery, 39
memory, 10, 115, 189
metacommunications, 34
mind and body, 80, 82, 84, 86, 88
mind-body unity, 85-86, 173
morale, 83
motivation, 55, 112, 158-159, 180, 194
Nancy School, 9-11, 48
Neo-Nancy school, 11-12
no-mind, 165-166
non-verbal, 75-76
orientation, 53, 72, 101-102, 125, 132-133, 145-146, 184
pain, 175-180
paradox, 34
perception, 88
perceptual-cognitive restructuring, 25
perceptual mode, 101-103, 106-108

Subject Index

personal equation, 80-81
phenomenology, 3, 74-75
phobias, 124, 127, 131, 187-193
placebo, 81-82
positive attitude, 174
positive unconscious, 44, 174, 189
pressure, 157-158
progressive relaxation, 162-163
re-education, 167, 183, 194
reinforcement, 125-127
relaxation, 38, 85, 107, 110, 111, 157, 162-163, 165, 172, 178, 184, 186-187, 189, 191, 194-195
reflexive attention, 13
regression, 159-160, 180-181, 190
resistance, 35, 137, 138-141
right brain, 69-73
role-taking theory, 24
Russian set theory, 60-62
self acceptance, 174
self esteem, 166-167
self- two self theory, 12
sensations, 67, 85, 88-89, 103-104, 109, 163-164, 178, 197
sensory awareness, 89-90
sleep theory, 21-22
state theory, 24
stress, 38, 66, 82-85, 101, 183-185, 186-187
   distress, 82, 175
   eustress, 82
suggestion, 37-55
   auto-suggestion, 11-15, 39-42, 46, 49

afferent, 46-48
binds, 30, 52, 173, 184
compound, 51, 172, 190, 192
contingent, 51, 170, 185
direct, 38, 46-48, 113, 164, 171
efferent, 46-48
hetero, 42
ideomotor, 44, 94
immediate, 46-48
open-ended, 49
implied directive, 171, 179, 186
indirect, 31, 38, 46-50, 62, 159, 172, 178, 179, 185, 192
indirect associative focusing, 50-51, 159-160, 161, 164, 171, 173, 186, 189-190
induced, 40-41, 171
mediate, 46-48
open-ended, 49, 161, 173, 179, 186
posthypnotic, 10, 52-53
spontaneous, 40-41
suggestibility, 53-55
susceptibility, 53-55
task, 54, 117, 134-136
time distortion, 115-120, 158-159, 180-183
thoughts, and self hypnosis, 9, 102-103, 93-94
trance, 97-120
   change with trance, 28-32, 153-198
   preparatory phase, 28-29, 99-103

ratification, 33, 105
therapeutic trance, 29, 32, 63, 65, 174-175, 182-183
thoughts, 188, 190
training, 97-98, 103-106
unconscious functioning, 62-63, 173, 174
utilization, 28, 31, 35
unconscious, 39, 42, 48, 57-77, 91, 98, 105, 106, 107, 114, 122, 126, 131, 132, 135-136
   abilities, 69, 98
   association, 63-65, 93, 123
   everyday unconscious, 58-59, 99-100
   intelligence, 57-58
   intuition, 60, 67-68
   knowing, 135-136, 172-173, 191
   language, 75-76
   learning, 58-59, 144-150, 182
   perception, 58
   peripheral associations, 100
   resistance, 137-144
   thinking, 63, 117-118, 127
verbal, 75-76
visualization, 92, 107, 110-112, 117-118, 127, 158, 160-162, 163, 165-166, 172, 180, 189, 191, 195
voluntary attention, 13, 110
warming, 97, 159, 178, 185-186

NOW AVAILABLE FROM IRVINGTON

VIDEO CASSETTES

DAVID GROVE AND B.I. PANZER
RESOLVING TRAUMATIC MEMORIES OF CHILD ABUSE: THE CASE OF SELWYN
A treatment for depression caused by child abuse. David Grove demonstrates new ways of resolving traumatic memories by evolving metaphors, 50 minutes.
Introductory price through 11/30/91—$65; $195 thereafter.

MICHAEL YAPKO
TRANCEWORK: A DEMONSTRATION OF HYPNOTIC PATTERNS
A sixty minute videotape illustrating basic principles and some of the different patterns inherent in the use of clinical hypnosis. Includes demonstrations of indirect induction, age regression, and glove anesthesia. *Michael Yapko* $225 (Color)

The Practice of Clinical Hypnosis
John G. Watkins

Forthcoming Fall 1991

VOL. I HYPNOTHERAPEUTIC TECHNIQUES
Volume I provides a background in the history of hypnosis, theories, suggestibility tests, induction, and deepening techniques. These are followed by chapters on suggestive methods of treatment within various branches of medicine. $39.50 0-8290-1462-4

VOL. II HYPNOANALYTIC TECHNIQUES
Volume II integrates hypnotic procedures with psychoanalytic and other "depth" therapies. The similarities and differences between psychoanalysis and hypnoanalysis are delineated, and a theoretical rationale provided to link the two. $39.50 0-8290-1463-2

VIDEO
HYPNOTIC PHENOMENA Demonstrates induction techniques and hypnotic phenomena including post hypnotic suggestions, perceptual distortions, hyperamnesia and regression, post hypnotic hallucinations and the hypnotic inculcation and resolution of an artificial neurosis. 90 minutes. *John G. Watkins* $300 (Color)

MIND BODY MEDICINE
by Lewis E. Mehl, M.D., PhD and Gayle H. Peterson, M.S.S.W.

Vol. I THE STAGES OF HEALING	$29.95	•⎕•
Vol. II THE LANGUAGE OF HEALING	$29.95	•⎕•

IRVINGTON PUBLISHERS, INC.
740 Broadway, New York, NY 10003

•⎕• includes audio cassette   Prices subject to change without notice. Prices higher outside the U.S.

NOW AVAILABLE FROM IRVINGTON

The Seminars, Workshops, and Lectures of Milton H. Erickson
Edited by Ernest L. Rossi and Margaret O. Ryan

Each volume contains rare photographs and an audio cassette of Erickson at work.

VOL. I HEALING IN HYPNOSIS
This is the first volume of Milton H. Erickson's seminars, workshops and lectures, edited in an informal manner to preserve his unique style of presentation.
$39.50   0-8290-0739-3

VOL. II LIFE REFRAMING IN HYPNOSIS
This volume describes Erickson's contribution to practical psychotherapy by showing the actual approaches, methods, and techniques that enable people to utilize their own experiences to change behavior and reframe their lives in meaningful ways.
$39.50   0-8290-1581-7

VOL. III MIND-BODY COMMUNICATION IN HYPNOSIS
This volume reflects the original views of Milton H. Erickson on psychosomatic medicine and healing, guiding the reader to a better understanding of hypnotherapeutic methods and the relationship between the mind and the body.
$39.50   0-8290-1805-0

VOL. IV CREATIVE CHOICE IN HYPNOSIS
This volume explores the following important questions through a presentation of Erickson's own hypnotic workshops and demonstrations. *Is hypnosis a process of manipulation or facilitation? Does the hypnotherapist control people? Or, does the hypnotherapist simply give clients permission to heal themselves?*

Available Summer 1991 $39.50   0-8290-2418-2

THE AUDIO SEMINARS, WORKSHOPS, AND LECTURES OF MILTON H. ERICKSON
The above 4 cassettes only—Price $49.95

ALSO AVAILABLE FROM IRVINGTON

EXPERIENCING HYPNOSIS: THERAPEUTIC APPROACHES $39.50
TO ALTERED STATES   0-8290-0246-4
    Milton Erickson & Ernest Rossi
HYPNOTHERAPY: AN EXPLORATORY CASEBOOK   0-8290-0244-8 $39.50
    Milton Erickson & Ernest Rossi
HYPNOTIC REALITIES: INDUCTION OF CLINICAL HYPNOSIS $29.95
AND FORMS OF INDIRECT SUGGESTION   0-8290-0112-3
    Milton Erickson, Ernest & Sheila Rossi
TIME DISTORTION IN HYPNOSIS   0-8290-0702-4 $29.50
    Linn F. Cooper & Milton Erickson

IRVINGTON PUBLISHERS, INC.
740 Broadway, New York, NY 10003

includes audio cassette   Prices subject to change without notice. Prices higher outside the U.S.

NOW AVAILABLE FROM IRVINGTON

ERICKSONIAN HYPNOTHERAPY VIDEOS

THE ARTISTRY OF MILTON H. ERICKSON In this two-part presentation, Milton H. Erickson elegantly demonstrates the clinical techniques in hypnosis that made his therapy so effective. 2 videos, 104 minutes. *Milton Erickson and Herbert Lustig* $400

A PRIMER OF ERICKSONIAN PSYCHOTHERAPY Recorded in professional television facilities, this thirty-two minute long videotape provides invaluable guidance to students of Erickson's clinical genius. *Milton Erickson and Herbert Lustig* $150

THE REVERSE SET IN HYPNOTIC INDUCTION A forty-five minute audio-visual presentation of a youthful Erickson. This is a valuable study of his earlier methods. *Milton Erickson* $185

All video cassettes are in color, except
The Reverse Set in Hypnotic Induction.

Please specify mode
BETA, VHS, or PAL

HYPNOTHERAPY AUDIO CASSETTES
BY JOHN AND HELEN WATKINS

HYPNOTIC INDUCTION TECHNIQUES by John G. Watkins. An instructional audio tape for the mental health professional. Recorded are live hypnotic inductions with explanatory narration including: arm drop suggestibility test, arm drop induction, hand levitation, repetitive movement, and subject object procedures. Running time, approximately 42 minutes.

RAISING SELF-ESTEEM by John and Helen H. Watkins. This tape is designed for mental health professionals to prescribe as "homework" for their patients to supplement regular therapy sessions. The tape is broken into two sections as "day tape side"—18 minutes, and "night tape side"—23 minutes.

All audio cassettes ordered separately are $14.00 each

IRVINGTON PUBLISHERS, INC.
740 Broadway, New York, NY 10003